A DEEPER PLACE

A DEEPER PLACE

Divine Vision for God's People

FLOYD BROWN II

ARPress
ILLUMINATING IDEAS.
EMPOWERING VOICES

All Scripture references are taken from the King James Version of the Bible.

Some names have been changed in *Until Now* to protect the innocent.

ARPress
45 Dan Road Suite 5
Canton MA 02021

Hotline: 1(800) 220-7660
Fax: 1(855) 752-6001

Ordering Information:
Quantity sales. Special discounts are available on quantity purchases by corporations, associations, and others. For details, contact the publisher at the address above.

Printed in the United States of America.

ISBN-13:	Paperback	979-8-89330-703-0
	eBook	979-8-89330-704-7
	Hardback	979-8-89330-705-4

Library of Congress Control Number: 2024901589

CONTENTS

TESTIMONIALS

My husband Floyd has the charisma, ability, and gift to encourage others. As his wife, I witness the essence of his life. Before he finished writing this book, he prayed intensely about it. I believe you will experience being motivated and inspired, and learn ways to discover deeper methods of connecting with God. I have personally experienced Floyd's words of encouragement, and they have deeply affected me and brought godly revelation to me. We all need a word of wisdom, whether we are Christians or not. Encouragement is vital, just as the air we breathe. Encouragement is contagious and is released to everyone else around you. It's beneficial for positive and internal change within everyone, and this is exactly what you will see and experience within these pages. This book contains compilations of literature Floyd has written for churches and online blogs after secret time in prayer. I have seen so many sisters and brothers encouraged and touched by God through his writings and godly messages.

Floyd is an introverted person; but guess what? He can preach! Once he is behind a pulpit, he is a totally different person because the Holy Spirit is with him. Also, he doesn't like to stay in crowded places. But when God called him to minister, he obeyed by becoming a leader in the church and making himself available to exhort and disciple its members. As his wife, I witnessed how, after he prays, he writes down a word of wisdom and encouragement. He has even awakened from his sleep to jot down prophetic messages from the Lord. When he wrote this book, he fully surrendered to God in prayer, hard work, and dedication to encourage the brethren. I'm so blessed as his wife and, of course, I am his number one fan.

Leah Jimenez-Brown

Floyd's ministry has been a very timely influence and encouragement in my ministry. He has called those things that are not as though they are, and many things have come to fruition. He has helped encourage me to preach, pastor, and reach souls. He encouraged me through dark times and fanned the fire for revival in nursing homes of all places. Last year, we saw nearly thirty people filled with the Holy Ghost and over twenty baptisms in Jesus' name, including a 103-year-old man in a nursing home. Floyd is a true man of God, and I'm honored to call him friend. Glory to God, I'm thankful for him.

Pastor Brock Hall

Prophet Floyd Brown is an honor to not just the Body of Christ, but to all. His heart and life are sold out to Jesus. Who he was before and who he is now is a testimony within itself: inspiring, encouraging, bringing forth God's Word for the true and living God! Because of who he is, this book will be beneficial in producing changed lives—lives that will impart God's truths to others, raising the name and the knowledge of Jesus Christ, and the prevailing of His Word. I give our God praise for him at such a time as this, as his journey takes him to a new dimension of service for the lives of awaiting multitudes! Prophet, you've only just begun.

Irene Magginson

DEDICATION

This book is dedicated to all newborn Christians, seasoned Christians, and Christian leaders. I wrote this book in an attempt to enable you to see yourself the way God sees you. It is presented as a tool of encouragement and exhortation for a variety of people within the Body of Christ. Our churches are in need of substantial measures of inspiration and dedication in order to establish God's kingdom on earth. Jesus said to accomplish the Great Commission as we seek to enlighten a sinful world (Matthew 28:16-20). But first, we must learn how to stand ourselves by deepening our relationships with God and enduring hardships as they arise. In order to show someone else how to endure, we must first endure.

I feel in my spirit that God is progressively moving toward strengthening His churches through His people. He is raising up some eagles. Some of you are in a transition right now, but God is changing something on the inside of you. He is positioning you to reach higher and dig deeper than ever before. Others have already soared, but God is getting ready to launch you into another level of purpose. By the Spirit of Jesus, I declare right now that God touches you right where you are and that He releases the anointing under which you were purposed to move. Hear what the Spirit of the Lord is searching for concerning you. Be one who will go for Him and will do all He requires of you. The goal of this book is to clearly share with you what God has given me to deliver to churches. I pray the Holy Spirit comforts many who are in need of a sense of reinforcement, revelation, and strengthening. Through these pages, I would like to offer a profound gesture of support and guidance in an effort to stimulate spiritual maturity within God's people.

FOREWORD

I met Prophet Floyd J. Brown in 2015 when I was going through our Calling & Ministry Studies (CAMS) program. I remember we were concluding our last session when two CAMS pastors walked around and prayed for each of the upcoming ministers. As we were ending with prayers, Brother Floyd had a great encounter with the Holy Spirit and God used him to prophesy to the entire class. It was definitely a moment when I believe God was in our midst, and I know without a shadow of a doubt that God was preparing us for our future ministries. Brother Floyd has a servant's heart and is willing to go the extra mile to help others. First Thessalonians 5:11 (NIV) says, *"Therefore encourage one another and build one another up, just as you are doing."* This verse resonates with me because we need more people to build up others rather than tear them down.

When Brother Floyd told me about this book, I was very excited for him and his enthusiasm to help others through difficult and perilous times. I know that this book will be a great encouragement, and that many lives will be touched. Brother Floyd is a great man of God, and he longs to reach a multi-cultural generation. His desire is to see people grow, have a godly experience, and to perhaps help change the world. This book is definitely a game-changer from which the next generation should glean, because everyone needs to have an encounter with Abba Father.

Elder Sandra M. Osborne

PREFACE

Throughout the years, I always admired those who wrote. It was an accomplishment I never imagined. In hindsight, God knew what He was about to do back in the year 2002. I was home in my little apartment, stricken with many afflictions and longing for a deep and devoted encounter with God Himself. It was a time in my life when all I had was God. Prayer was my resting place, and receiving a touch from God was my absolute pursuit. One day after prayer, I was led to Habakkuk 2:1, which says:

> *I will take my stand at my watchpost and station myself on the tower, and look out to see what He will say to me, and what I will answer concerning my complaint. And the LORD answered me, and said, **write the vision**, and make it plain upon tables, that he may run that readeth it.*

And so for some calculated reason, God urged me to preserve this verse over many years. He also advised me to write down messages and begin distributing them to various people. This godly project was more than I ever expected. You see, seven years later, God convinced me to go back to school to study for six years. After all the grueling essays and academic projects, I became someone who loved to write. Even more, I was a man who loved God and sought to write down everything He commanded me to write. I began to file old messages I had written, while often writing new ones. Over time, I accumulated material I had written that I knew could be structured into a book—messages that had been used for encouragement, exhortation, and preaching. It was deep revelation God imparted to me when I needed it, and wisdom that only God Himself could have revealed in the midst of trials and troubles. All these messages are presented in this book to give you a greater sense of hope and inspiration. It is because I love God's church that I also show my support. More than anything, God wants the hearts of His people. So, in this book, I not only bring divine insight to you from what's been poured into my spirit over a long period of time, but I also pour out God's heart to you.

INTRODUCTION

I t is said that in order to fly, you must first take a leap. No society or organization can ever accomplish their mission without first opening their doors and making substantial efforts toward developing into what they have envisioned. Additionally, detailed strategies would certainly be put in place to overcome a variety of obstacles in order to progress as an industry and/or organization. In the same way, as Christians, we are inspired to accomplish our missions by stimulating faith and taking the necessary steps forward to pursue God's direction and counsel over our lives. Within that process, we learn to apply spiritual tactics that help our maturity processes and manage our difficulties more fluently. Without a doubt, God has strategy and a keen path of vision for those who seek it.

A lifelong journey can often be uncertain. Accomplishments are usually combined with failures, lessons learned, and extremities of life. However, the fact is that we, as mankind, live only by God's divine mercy, as we seek to discover our true identities while living out the existence a mighty God has given us. Nevertheless, as mere humans, God has made Himself available to us through the Scriptures, through His presence, and through the breath He purposefully breathed within us (Genesis 2:7). In this way, we see a glimpse of hope even in the darkest moments of life. We sense a God that is determined to draw us near unto Him throughout the entire course of our lives.

Yet, on the other hand, we are stricken with adversities which the enemy, Satan, seeks to use to terminate our godly purposes. It is a demonic operation attempting to disrupt our predetermined connections with God. This is often identified as a constant battle against the flesh—spiritually aided by the remorseless influence of the principalities of darkness. Nevertheless, the God who gave us life seeks to preserve life and encourage us to succeed. As it is written, Jesus came into the world to seek and to save that which was lost and to demonstrate His love for all mankind—regardless of our frailties, uncertainties, and hardships. There is absolute hope in Jesus (Luke 19:10). To make things even better, God has given His people empowerment—strategies to overcome fear, defeat, aimlessness, and despair. The more we seek His divine direction, the more we see the hand of God unfold before our eyes.

Chapter 1

GOD IS NEAR

Each day, mankind seeks a sense of fulfillment in this world. However, many will tell you that seeking contentment in the world has proven to be disappointing. While in sin, we all, at one time or another, have sought after earthly satisfaction, aimlessly nurturing our lifestyles and blindly indulging our souls. It is a continuous downward spiral that never succeeds in producing either satisfaction or fulfillment for us. In the end, nothing can ever satisfy the soul, or perhaps preserve life more, than the Creator who made it. God gives life to what did not exist before.

In the book of Genesis, the text specifies that God breathed the breath of life into mankind, and the body and soul came **alive.** Genesis 2:7 says, *"And the LORD God formed man of the dust of the ground, and breathed into his nostrils the breath of life; and man became a living soul."*

You see, even though mankind received God's presence first, mankind has continually sought after everything apart from God and His true purpose for their lives. However, God is not hidden from us unless we choose our own way. But, those who wholeheartedly seek after Him shall find Him. Proverbs 8:17 says, *"I love them that love me; and those that **seek me** shall **find me**."* Likewise, the Word also says, *"**Seek**, and **you will find**; **knock**, and it will be **opened to you**"* (Matthew 7:7). Meet God where He pursues you. Just imagine if you had a child whom you sought after and observed each day. But their backs were always towards you and they never acknowledged you or even sought to spend time with you. Well that's how God feels about His creation. We are made in His image (Genesis 1:27). He has a heart. He has feelings. He has a desire for connection. That's why He made you.

For those of you who have not already found God, consider making a sensible choice today. Allow God to lead your life now. Tomorrow never has a promise waiting for you without God. He is the God of life, and *all* life stems from Him. Make sure you have experienced a genuine encounter with the God that created you. Be near to God, as He has chosen to be near to you since the beginning of time. James 4:8 says, ***"Draw near*** *to God as He* ***draws near*** *to you."* In that truth, our lives will be complete as God continues to breathe upon our lives by releasing the outpouring of His profound existence and the direction of His infallible counsel. In these last days, God has been searching for the hearts of His people through His undeniable presence. Acts 2:17 says, *"'In the last days,' God says, I will* ***pour out*** *my Spirit upon all people."* It does not end there. Each day forward is an opportunity to gain access to a divine power that knows you by name and calls you His very own. As we receive this gift, we find out through the eyes of God how He meticulously sees us. As we encounter this unconditional gesture of acceptance, we discover the true reason for our existence. Yet, life is contingent upon our decisions. When we choose to satisfy our souls without the vanity of a human mindset, we renew our minds with a divine connection with the Creator. This is exactly what we were created for.

God Searches for You

The Lord has fashioned us in a way that allows us to retain our own free will by assuming our desires—ultimately determining our own paths. That's one reason the Scripture says, *"Above all, guard the heart, for out of it are the issues of life"* (Proverbs 4:23). Many distractions exist that may hinder us from a divine connection with God.

Nevertheless, there is a better way. Despite those realities, God faithfully intends to lead mankind toward the narrow way of eternal life, through the hope and redemption of salvation by the blood Jesus Christ shed upon the cross. Regardless of the interferences and adversities of this world, Jesus has promised hope in the face of it all (Luke 23:44-46).

Still mankind, for thousands and thousands of years, has sought after everything except God's mind and heart. Instead, they have pursued their own selfish desires and pleasures. Galatians 5:19-21 says:

> *Now the works of the flesh are evident: sexual immorality, impurity, sensuality, idolatry, sorcery, enmity, strife, jealousy, fits of anger, rivalries, dissensions, divisions, envy, drunkenness, orgies, and things like these. I warn you, as I warned you before, that those who do such things will not inherit the kingdom of God.*

As a result of sin, every so often, God allows unfavorable circumstances to take place in one's life. Many people will particularly encounter a strong sense of emptiness from within themselves—causing them to self-reflect and closely examine their lifestyle. Yet through mercy, God constantly reveals His love and concern for humanity. You see, because we have our own free will to decide our lives and seek to determine our own paths, God has a way of searching our hearts and examining our minds (Jeremiah 17:10). Psalm 53:2 says, *"God looks down from heaven on the children of man to see if there are any who understand, who seek after God."* In this way, we are given a choice to submit to God's divine authority, but it always remains a choice. It is a critical one; it is an opportunity to give honor and reverence to our Creator of life itself. Therefore, it is imperative to be mindful of God's course of action, direction, instructions, and warnings.

Furthermore, we must be careful how we demonstrate obedience and allegiance to Him. Suppose we were to self-reflect and see what our hearts and minds are determined to do, and where our internal agendas are directed. This, of course, would help us to see if we are focused on God's heart and God's divine purpose for our lives.

How often do we internally examine ourselves?

Are our lifestyles in accordance to God's Word?

Do we seek after the heart of God?

Have we displayed obedience to God?

How often do we refuse God's instructions and His direction for our lives?

Has God tugged at our hearts about a certain issue for correction?

2 Timothy 3:16 says, *"All Scripture is breathed out by God and profitable for teaching, for reproof, for correction, and for training in righteousness, so that the servant of God may be thoroughly equipped for every 'good' work."* Every good work, actions that honor God, show hearts and minds that seek the mind of God and His agendas—not just our own desires. Where are our hearts today? Have we committed our hearts to God's heart? Serve God like never before. Pursue His heart deeper than you ever sought before. Reach for God's presence more than you ever imagined you could. Know Him more closely than you knew Him yesterday. God has a yearning heart for His people.

God's Heart

The core of God's heart begins with the cross. God masterfully provided a way of redemption for humanity after the fall of man and sin. He presented Jesus (God the Son) as a sacrificial demonstration of His love for a world of near doom and destruction. His method has generated hope for us all and caused us to see what we were always meant to accomplish in life. In this pursuit of life, God's desire for His people is to take up their crosses and to seek after His presence with all diligence. The cross is where God gave mankind a second chance to acknowledge His Lordship and adhere to His vision for us all, yearning for His presence at all times and sustaining close relations with Him. In this way, we not only prevent what is contrary to Him from happening, but we keep a close connection to God's timing and His movements throughout the earth. Exodus 23:12 tells us, *"And now, Israel (people of God), what does the Lord your God require of you, but to fear the Lord your God, to walk in all his ways, to love him, to serve the Lord your God with **all your heart** and with **all your soul**."* Ephesians 5:10 also commands, *"And try to discern what is **pleasing** to the Lord."*

Making sure we are exactly where God has purposed us to be is paramount. To truly be a part of God's vision, we are often divinely led and connected to healthy church settings with sound doctrine. And as we lift up His eternal name, in God's house is where true identity begins to flourish. It is in God's house where God uses us in some way to reveal the capacity of our godly purposes. More to the point, it is significant for us as God's people to be participants of something greater than ourselves, for the sake of Christ. It's not tolerating idleness or complacency in ourselves, but being willing to contribute to the enhancement of church functions where there is an apparent need. Clearly, this is, of course, where God's heart resides—the place where we surrender our all for an unselfish cause. And being a part of something greater than ourselves urges God to prove Himself and demonstrate His work in our lives.

Unsurprisingly, although all people are not called to be ministers or evangelists, we are still called to reach out to the lost. This is a critical endeavor, as we lead others to their only hope in this life that God has given them through salvation in Christ. Matthew 24:14 says, *"And this gospel of the kingdom will be proclaimed throughout the whole world as a testimony to all nations, and then the end will come."* Mark 16:15 says,

"And he said to them, 'Go into the entire world and proclaim the gospel to the whole creation.'" Therefore, we must not be silent as witnesses in any country or region. Proclaim Christ in all parts of the earth, as God is well-pleased with this. There is always someone around us who needs to hear about the splendor of Jesus. When we reach out to others, we are alleviating discouragement and allowing God to do His work on earth as He has declared to do through His people.

Just image if you were used of God to go out into the streets; the malls, the homeless shelters, neighborhoods, etc. And picture a man or woman you approach as you hand them some literature about Jesus. Then you eventually walk away and you never see that person again. Well, you see, God uses you to drop a seed and then later He waters that seed. What if, that person you gave a religious track to went home and about a few months later contemplated on committing suicide? So they pick up a gun or some pills and then suddenly they think about the literature you were led of God to present to them. God has a method to saving lives and you might somehow be a part of that. This is a vital initiative. God's heart is yearning for His movement in the churches, but we must make ourselves available to be of service. In such cases of participation, God will methodically do His wonderful works among His people. Signs, wonders and miracles will follow those who are sincere seekers of the divine (Mark 16:17-18, KJV). In other words, God has declared that He who seeks after Him shall surely find Him (Matthew 7:7, NIV). In addition, those who once lived in darkness will have the glory of God's light shine upon their faces. Lives that were, at one time, in captivity and despair will be set free.

It is imperative that we don't just settle for life as usual. You have got to **expect** the move of God. The revivals that are most **impactful** are the ones where churches jointly reached out in **unity** expecting something special to happen, determined to experience a divine encounter with God. **Settling** for church as usual is only a limited portion of God's presence among His people. Don't just **settle** for God on the surface. Search for God in the deep. When we come *expecting* the move of God,

He *will* move in our midst. The Bible says in Jeremiah 29:11, *"For **I know** the **thoughts** that **I think towards you**, saith the LORD, **thoughts** of **peace**, and **not** of **evil**, to **give you** an **expected end**."* Expect God to move when you have done your part. Acts 2:1-2 says: *"When the day of Pentecost came, they were all together in one place (expecting). And suddenly there came from heaven a sound like a **mighty rushing wind**, and it **filled** the entire house where they were sitting."*

The deepest connections with God are the ones where His people **dig deep** and **reach higher**. Irrefutably, deep and desperate hearts move God. All these things are at the core of God's heart. We must do our part to please Him. Life is not all about what we desire; it's about what God desires for us. We live today and we die tomorrow. We can spend our whole lives pleasing ourselves, and it takes us nowhere. But when we live to please God, He takes us places nothing or no one else can fulfill. Live to please God in all you do. Set your mind on more of what God desires of you, rather than what you desire for yourself.

Pursue the Heart of God

When you focus on God's heart, you are bound to end up in the throne room. Our intentions are never to offend God, but only to allow Him to be a significant feature of our lives. However, a portion of our churches are falling short of operating at their fullest potential. The point is that God has a role for us to participate in within the Body of Christ. You see, serving God is not only about attending church functions. Instead, it's about functioning at the capacity God has given you. So the questions are these:

1) Who are you really purposed to be?
2) Do you know what your calling is for the Lord?
3) Have you been Spirit-filled?
4) Are you sure that God has revealed to you how you are to function in life and in the church?

If the answer is no to any of these questions, it is paramount that we pursue the heart of God to ascertain that we are exactly where God purposed us to be. Of course, not everyone is called to be in the pulpit. Yet, God's people are absolutely purposed to be a part of the church in order to assist in the building of God's house. In fact, there are several members within our reach every Sunday who still may not know what they are called to do or where God's purpose for them leads. In such instances, our churches will not grow into the healthy and mature congregations in which God intended for these individuals to operate. The bottom line is that if our churches do not move out of their sense of complacency, they will not fulfill their assigned destinies. This means to be genuinely and actively seeking after what God created us for, rather than what we have created for ourselves. If we adhere to God's heart, the move of God will flourish in our lives more than we ever imagined.

So I urge you today—make sure that you as a member of your local church can identify with what you are purposed to do to demonstrate your allegiance and service to God. When you see His face, will God say that you have done all He called you to do? Will God be able to say that your heart was focused on His agenda instead of your own? Be sure that, in the end, nothing is more fulfilling than knowing what you were purposed for in the eyes of God. Remaining firm in God is accomplished not only by church attendance and the words we speak, but typically by our actions that result in God's pleasure. Stand in the gap. We are ultimately on earth to connect with God and to carry out His purposes. Let us awaken, arise, and stand for God in our hearts, not just attending church because we should, or perhaps only to receive a blessing. Some enjoy the social aspects of church. However, seeking after the righteousness of God and making ourselves available to be used by the power of the Holy Spirit is the essence of functioning properly as a church. Moreover, let us reach out to help those who are entangled with the darkness of this world, ensuring we have done all to discover our divine assignments on earth.

Awaken, arise, and stand in this fight between good and evil. The fact is that whether you choose to battle for the Lord or not, the enemy Satan will still seek to destroy us all. John 10:10 says, *"The thief (Satan) comes to steal and kill and destroy. My purpose is to give them a rich and satisfying life."* For that reason, make your stance count in your journey with the Lord, without any form of reservation, slothfulness, or complacency. Ascertain that you have **measured your heart** to see if it is truly in the faith and that you are not conformed to this wicked and immoral world system. Clearly, in this life, many challenges exist. We are born into a world of confusion and chaos. Nevertheless, God has offered meaningfulness and purpose through such harsh conditions. In fact, He valued us in a way only He can fully describe through His word. God says, *"Declaring the end from the beginning and from ancient times things not yet done, saying, 'My counsel shall stand, and I will accomplish all my purpose'"* (Isaiah 46:10).

Fortunately, God has given us assurance that no matter what circumstances we face in life, He will vindicate us in the end. Awaken, arise, and stand to be certain that God is glorified through your efforts, and you have genuinely lived and died not to just please yourself, but to glorify God. The question is, are we willing to be close to God, even during difficulty? How close do you want to be with God? A Sunday morning service? A Bible study? A ten-minute prayer? The fact is that there is much more to our salvation to encounter than just that.

1) God is searching for those who are hungry enough for Him, despite their encounters with hardship (James 1:2-4).
2) God is searching for laborers to be a witness for Him—reaching out, revealing hope to a dark world of chaos and confusion (Acts 1:8).
3) God is searching for a people who will commit themselves to building up His church, developing into a church that will become mature, attaining to the whole measure of the fullness of Christ (Ephesians 4:11-13).

4) God is searching for a church without spot or wrinkle—
   proclaiming unity, holiness, and empowerment (Ephesians 5:27).

5) God is searching for people that are willing to diligently seek
   after His presence—not only seeking when they are in need of
   something (Proverbs 8:17).

Overall, let us consider our relationship with God. He is the
beginning and the end of all things, the one who spoke us into existence
and it was done. *"Many plans are in a man's heart, But the counsel of the
Lord will stand"* (Proverbs 19:21).

Seeking God Closely

How much do you want to know God closely? To know God closely
is to deeply pursue Him. It means valuing our time with Him above
all else. A person can live his/her whole life without knowing God—
without even touching the surface of His glory. But there is a depth
in God, and we can only encounter that depth through seeking His
presence during heartfelt prayer, keenly meditating on biblical truths,
or selflessly allowing God to use us as vessels for His kingdom.

So I ask again, how much do you want to know God closely? How
many of us could establish a deep relationship with our loved ones in
just a few minutes, or without time and effort? For instance, if we spend
only fifteen to twenty minutes with our husbands and wives per day,
our relationships would be in jeopardy. We must consider knowing
God the same way. Time spent with God getting to know Him is
not just a five- to ten-minute prayer; it's not just quoting one or two
Scriptures or attending church on Sundays and doing nothing else to
pursue Him during the week. Knowing God closely requires **desire** and
time. It involves **hunger, thirst, reaching, digging, lengthening,** and
developing our time with God—perhaps like we never have before.
Matthew 5:6 says, *"Blessed are those who hunger and thirst for God's
approval. They will be satisfied."* John 6:35 says, *"Jesus said to them, 'I am*

the bread of life; he who comes to Me will not hunger, and he who believes in Me will never thirst.'"

I want to explain what happens when we are serious enough to chase after God until the manifestation of His presence is undeniable. First of all, God has formed and marked us all to know Him closely and to love Him. It is His absolute desire to see us long for Him and establish an intensely devoted relationship with Him. In that, we know that He is ***accessible*** and ***not far away*** from those who pursue Him.

Let me give you an example of something I encountered. In the year 2000, I was a member of a small church in Baltimore, Maryland. One particular day, we attended the Sunday morning church service, and the congregation enjoyed the presence of God. We all had a good time with the Lord. Later that day, I returned for the evening service only to find that no one else had shown up. I headed inside to confirm, and my mentor, Elder Andrew Henry, who was a pastor at that time, greeted me and said, "No one else showed up for Sunday night church service; let us pray." We then began to pray—the pastor on one side of the room and I on the other.

As we bowed down before God in prayer, we reached out deeper unto God—to the point where we were walking around the church with our hands in the air, exalting God and reaching for His presence. After forty to forty-five minutes went by, all of a sudden, the very divine presence of God manifested in a profound way—causing us to not be able to stand in God's presence. We had to bow down at His glory! It was as if God was standing right next to me. A very warm and powerful presence lingered for about fifteen seconds, then it withdrew. Then the pastor looked up at me from the other side of the room and said, "Did you feel that awesome presence of God?" In shock, I replied, "Yes."

In my mind, I thought to myself, *I wish that presence hadn't gone away.* Then God spoke right to me and said, "Who said I was gone?" Immediately, the awesome presence of God returned...and it lingered for another ten to twelve seconds. Identical to my experience, the pastor explained to me that he was also standing and felt that God's presence was so glorious that he had to bow down.

So, you see, there are different levels of God's presence. And if we limit or neglect our time with God, we miss out on the depth of His glory and the deepest meaning of knowing Him. If we are longing for the deep things of God, just realize that He is waiting to draw us close to Him and to manifest Himself in our lives in ways we have not experienced before. There is no limit to God's glory. How much do you want to know Him closely? Reach for God—chase after His presence.

Encouragement to the God Chaser

Searching for closeness with God has its rewards. In the midst of our walk with God, He has orchestrated a plan for us, "The God Chaser." His plan is to dip us into the depth of His divine presence and shield us with victory! In difficult moments, He walks closely with us through the fire, but we are not scorched. He plunges us into the deep waters, and we are not overtaken.

> *When you pass through the waters, I will be with you; and through the rivers, they shall not overwhelm you; when you walk through the fire you shall not be burned, and the flame shall not consume you.* (Isaiah 43:2)

*Beloved, think it not strange concerning the fiery trial which is to try you, as though some strange thing happened unto you. But rejoice inasmuch as you participate in the sufferings of Christ, so that you may be overjoyed when **His glory is revealed**.* (1 Peter 4:12-13)

Unfortunately, with or without God, suffering comes in many forms throughout our lives. Even in the midst of it, we must understand the meaning of true happiness and what is most essential in life.

1 Peter 5:10 says, *"And the God of all grace, who called you to his eternal glory in Christ, after you have suffered a little while, will himself restore you and make you strong, firm and steadfast."*

2 Corinthians 1:3-4 tells us, *"Praise be to the God and Father of our Lord Jesus Christ, the Father of compassion and the God of all comfort, who comforts us in all our troubles, so that we can comfort those in any trouble with the comfort we ourselves receive from God."*

Romans 8:18 says, *"I consider that our present sufferings are not worth comparing with the glory that will be revealed in us."*

The man named Job who lost everything, including his family and his health, said, *"Though he slay me, I will trust him"* (Job 13:15) and *"Naked I came into the world and naked I go out...The name of the Lord will still be praised!"* (Job 1:21). As a result, Job was doubly blessed for his trouble when God restored him. If only we would just depend on God...while depending on and trusting in God, we will eventually find that every piece of the puzzle has been divinely manipulated by His hand. He forces us to rest in Him so that we will learn to trust Him. To trust God is to ultimately know God. In knowing God, we find helpful characteristics of discipline, wisdom, strength, tenacity, and contentment. Those are the benefits of chasing after God. Proverbs 3:5-6 exhorts us to, *"Trust in the Lord with all your heart; and lean not unto your own understanding. In all your ways acknowledge Him and He will direct thy path."* James 5:10 tells us, *"As an example of suffering and patience, brothers, take the prophets who spoke in the name of the Lord."*

There is no one who does not suffer some level of difficulty. It, of course, is not a sin to suffer, but to live in sin while suffering is a problem. Basically, if you are prosperous in life, that does not make you sinless; and if you are not prosperous, that does not necessarily make you a sinner. Matthew 5:45 says, *"That ye may be the children of your Father which is in heaven: for he maketh his sun to rise on the evil and on the good, and sendeth rain on the **just** and on the **unjust.**"* So, even when we go through extreme experiences, God is still with us and very near. It is written in God's Word, *"Do not be afraid or discouraged, for the Lord will go before you and will be with you; He will neither fail you nor abandon you"* (Deuteronomy 31:8). 1 Peter 3:14 also tells us, *"But even if you should suffer for what is right, you are blessed. Do not fear their threats; do not be frightened."*

God chaser! As we trust and relentlessly reverence God, know God is faithful. Most of all, let us keep in mind that there are unequivocally no constraints to His glory—His divine intervention has absolute power over our circumstances. Therefore, in the midst of adversity, we must continue to chase Him with all our heart, soul, mind, and strength! Narrow down the chase and avoid the deception of spiritual slothfulness and complacency.

Complacency

God has fashioned mankind to identify with who He is. He has promised to preserve us in His critical and essential role as creator in every phase of our lives. It is at the deepest portion of God's heart to see His people desire Him. Proverbs 8:17 says, *"I love them that love me; and those that seek me shall find me."* Jeremiah 29:13 promises, "You will *seek me* and *find Me when* you *seek Me* with *all your heart.*" In fact, there is a fine line between complacency and religion. God doesn't want us to be complacent, and He doesn't want us to *just* be religious. He desires a deep and genuine relationship with each and every one of us. More to the point, it's not just about attending church, but it includes reaching for God from our hearts with a sense of intensity. That means not being complacent with religious ritual, but finding God on a different level than just a short prayer or a Sunday church service.

Life is short...have we sought after and sincerely reached out to discover the depth of God? Are we sure that we have given God our absolute, undivided attention? Have we allowed the hand of God to take full control of our lives? Have we sincerely lived to uphold the things of God and totally insisted on pleasing Him? Have we stepped outside of our daily comfort zone of complacency for the Lord? Avoiding complacency is essential. In general, it is when we emphasize doing whatever pleases the heart of God, finding out exactly who we are purposed to be in the sight of God, and aligning ourselves properly enough to prevent moments of hindrance and distraction. For that reason, Colossians 3:2 says, *"Set your heart on things above, not on things on the earth."* Most importantly, this world can neither save us nor completely satisfy us because we were strategically created to please God...and if we leave this earth today, **would we be able** to say that we have done all we possibly could to please God? Could we say that we are in search of our God-given purposes? Well, let us consider avoiding complacency and begin to allow God to reveal Himself and move swiftly in our lives. Any pursuit without God's purpose for our finite existence is vanity.

Chapter 2

THE VANITY OF MANKIND

Many challenges, influences, and obstacles are too often present in this world. When we are young, we are searching for social acceptance and stability. In my early years, I pursued many things that were satisfying only for a few years. I was somewhat of a troubled teen; I partied, chased and dated many beautiful women, participated in bodybuilding, studied martial arts for years, joined the United States Marines, served in law enforcement, and achieved higher education by obtaining a master's degree. Yet, none of these pursuits were completely fulfilling, and my life never met its true purpose.

Apart from my experience, I knew a decorated military serviceman who was a well-known sheriff deputy. He was also a fifth-degree black belt in martial arts. He went to Iraq during a war and died within two weeks. You see, the fact is that we live only by God's mercy...so it does not matter how many skills we have, how strong we are, or how much knowledge we obtain. The only thing that truly matters is God's undeniable presence. In fact, the first thing that mankind received was God's presence (Genesis 1:26-27), and that is the very thing mankind has forgotten or walked away from in this world. Without a doubt, the only thing that ever made a significant difference in my life was being in God's presence—identifying with my true purpose through Him. Many times people believe they are exactly where they belong, but there is only one true purpose through the God who created you. Seeking God and pursuing Him to determine who we really are is paramount.

Discovering what God has planned for us can change the atmosphere of our surroundings. This is known as an epiphany—encountering a divine experience with God that only He can produce.

Interestingly, but not surprisingly, the richest man in biblical history, King Solomon, who had everything at his fingertips, said in Ecclesiastes 12:13, *"Let us hear the conclusion of the whole matter: Fear God, and keep his commandments: for this is the whole duty of man."* Naturally, he realized that people fade away like the grass, but God and His Word lasts forever. Solomon came to realize that nothing in this world could ever satisfy him the way God could. In that, he found a strong sense of purpose and direction. He acknowledged that God offered a deeper meaning to life and ultimately discovered mankind's true identity.

Identity in Christ

To be able to meet God right where we are in life is a profound gesture of His love. Despite the sinfulness of mankind that stems from many generations, God still today offers compassion and unconditional support to those who receive Him.

> *For the sin of this one man, Adam, caused death to rule over many. But even greater is God's wonderful grace and his gift of righteousness, for all who receive it will live in triumph over sin and death through this one man, Jesus Christ.* (Romans 5:17)

> *But he who unites himself with the Lord is one with him in spirit.* (1 Corinthians 6:17)

> *Therefore being justified by faith, we have peace with God through our Lord Jesus Christ.* (Romans 5:1)

> *For ye were bought with a price: therefore glorify God in your body, and in your spirit, which are God's.* (1 Corinthians 6:20)

But you are a chosen people, a royal priesthood, a holy nation, a people belonging to God, that you may declare the praises of him who called you out of darkness into his wonderful light. (1 Peter 2:9)

Finding your calling in life is essential. Without purpose, mankind is lost in the vanity of life. According to 2 Timothy 3:7, man is, *"Always learning and never able to arrive at a knowledge of the truth."* True purpose involves knowing exactly what God wants you to do in your physical and spiritual life. Being made in God's image, each individual is created by God for a specific purpose. Genesis 1:27 says, *"So God created man in his own image, in the image of God he created him; male and female he created them."* Decades later, God put aside all His power and glory and dwelt among us in the flesh (1 John 4:2) as Jesus Christ to make evident how much He sought after our love toward Him, to emphasize to us how much He cared for us. Additionally, He wanted to show us how to live. This was done ultimately so that we could find our true purpose through Him.

Know Your True Purpose

The purposes of God are closely linked to knowing our divine callings. Believers have a genuine hope to find whatever purpose God has for us through the leading of His Spirit. However, it's unfortunate that those who do not serve God have a more difficult time finding their true purpose. I was raised by my parents in a Holy Ghost-filled Pentecostal church in Baltimore, Maryland. Then at age thirteen, I began to drift away from the things of God. Even though I was attending church with my family, my focus became socializing and interacting with other teens in the church. As I fell even further away from God, I became a troubled teen and began hanging out in the streets, trying to fit in. Even worse, I stopped attending church. By age eighteen, I remember living a disobedient life of vanity and confusion.

One day, a close friend named Darick Harris asked me to meet him at a house party. To make a long story short, a fight broke out in front of the house in the street. Darick was shot along with two other friends of mine, Charles Jones and Anthony Holman. Simultaneously, I and several others were also being fired upon and we were forced to duck between cars and trees. I went home that night with Darick's blood on my face. The next day, Sunday morning, Darick died. But I thank God for the opportunity He gave Darick during the last critical moments of his life. After Darick was shot, he was rushed to the hospital. And once he was able to regain consciousness a priest came in the room to visit him and pray with him. Darick prayed the sinner's prayer and asked Jesus into his life. Shortly after, he passed away.

My close friend's death was a life-changing moment for me—one that brought about a lot of soul-searching. My hanging-out days ended. I began to focus on a career and decided to join the United States Marines. Finally, at age twenty-four, I enlisted and found myself in a world of adversity through the United States Marine boot camp training. Being punched and spit on by drill instructors, we recruits experienced hard lives. In these moments during training, I once again recognized the significance of needing God in our lives. I sometimes held a cross in my hands before going to bed. If anybody ever tells you that military enlistees don't seek God, don't believe them. They do, often simply because they are going through tough times.

Three months after Marine Corps boot camp ended for me, I found out that one of my drill instructors that graduated my platoon shot himself in front of fifty-six recruits on their sixth day of training at the swim qualification.[1] At that point, I did some self-reflection in relation to my true purpose in life. I realized that drill instructor was in some way supposed to be a mentor—yet internally he had no peace or true direction in whatever he was going through in his life. None of

---

[1]   Anonymous (1994). *Marine Drill Instructor Kills Self in Front of Recruits.* AP News. Retrieved September 25, 2019 from https://apnews.com/ebc8f2efd018e40 d504fd096e1dbb22d.

us recruits knew he was suffering from Post-Traumatic Stress Disorder (PTSD) from the 1990 Saudi War. Yet, at times I would often emulate him, but something was missing. Still, I continued to live my life without seeking God—and without any further consideration of my past experiences, church roots, or Christian beliefs. However, when I turned age thirty, everything changed.

One day, I was watching the 1999 movie, "The Ten Commandments." All of a sudden, I felt the presence of God. Being raised up in church, I knew what that presence felt like. Tears rolled down my face. Then, for the first time ever, I heard God's voice. He said, "I want to use you the same way I used Moses." "I want to use you to help and strengthen My people." I replied to God that I was not capable of being used in that way. God's presence lingered until He finally spoke to me. "Enough is enough...it's time for you to know who you really are. You have wallowed in your mistakes long enough. You got all that play out of you. I'm calling you out of this world; I'm calling you into ministry. Your true purpose is not being a United States Marine; your true purpose is not being a police officer. You are a man of God. I am not calling you into the warfare of the land, but I am calling you into the warfare of the air."

The Bible says, *"Our weapons of warfare are not carnal, but mighty through God, for the pulling down of strongholds"* (2 Corinthians 10:4). In other words, one's life is contingent upon spiritual matters—how we deal with evil influences that oppose God's divine plan for mankind. Spiritual weapons of warfare are utilized in the spiritual realm while mankind's weapons are used in the natural world. For God's people, we are heavenly equipped with impactful prayer and profound ordinances of God's Word to combat against spiritual forces. We are created to proclaim the manifestation of God's power and the supernatural authority that stems from it. I answered that call on my life.

Many people may not know what their true purpose or calling is today, but I am here to tell you that God wants to show you who you really are. *"He that began a great work in you (even when He created you) is able to complete you until the end"* (Philippians 1:6). We were all created to do great things through God. God has planted something special inside all of us. We are all created for a specific purpose—uniquely made. So I encourage you, know who you are. Know your true purpose. Find out what God has in store for you.

There Is Another You

Without a doubt, you may have always been sustained through the various phases of your life: internally, financially, and socially. But do you **really** know who you are? You decisively look forward to acquiring achievements and to somehow benefit from every aspect of life; your life is filled with personal goals and harsh deadlines. But do you know who you really are in God's eyes and what you were really meant to pursue? God seeks to develop another you within you. No matter who you are right now or what you have become, there is still another you. The truth is, God sees in you a person with a greater potential—ultimately created to live out a meaningful life through a God-given purpose. With the many obstacles and various distractions of life, we are often hindered from becoming what God truly created us to be. Ecclesiastes 7:29 says, *"Behold, I have found only this, that God made men upright, but they have sought out many devices."*

In other words, God has made us to be godly people, but mankind has sought after many other things apart from what God has designed for us. Yet God is not hidden from us, and He is often willing to manifest the glory He has formed in us. Isaiah 43:6-8 says, *"I will say to the north, 'Give them up!' And to the south, 'Do not hold them back.' Bring My sons from afar and My daughters from the ends of the earth, Bring out the people who are blind, even though they have eyes, And the deaf, even though they have ears."* Do we have eyes to see where God wants to take us? Do we have ears to hear what God is impressing upon us to do? There is another you...a you that was created to be stimulated by the hand of God and His power...a you that has been ordained for God and His divine purpose in your life…a you that brings out the best in you the way God intended it to be. Job 33:4 says, *"The Spirit of God has made me, and the breath of the Almighty gives me life."*

So, today, I challenge you to determine to discover the true purpose God has for you. Avoid the things of this world or anything that is designed by evil to hinder that purpose of God in your life. Clearly, nothing is more fulfilling or significant in life than to know your true purpose. God says there is more than what is on the surface. If you reach higher for Him, you will certainly discover the real purpose you are for your life. Never be complacent. ***There is more*** to who you really are in the hand of God. There are underlying reasons for our existence. No one was ever created by God to be either ordinary or irrelevant. In fact, no matter where you are in life, no matter how many obstacles you face, no matter how anxious you may feel, there is greatness in you. You were created to encounter God's divine purpose and to overcome the adversities of this world. More to the point, you were born for a specific mission, which is to please God. And before God formed you in the womb, He had your life purposed for a great path just waiting to be revealed through His perfect work. Ephesians 1:4-5 says, *"For he chose us in him before the creation of the world to be holy and blameless in his sight. In love he predestined us for adoption as sons through Jesus Christ, according to the purpose of his will."*

In other words, we were predestined for our steps to be ordered by the Lord and to live out the plan God has for us. It involves commitment in pursuing God's heart's desire for our lives and, ultimately, discovering exactly who we were created to be by seeing it literally unfold before our eyes. In this world, there are many distractions, challenges, and uncertainties. Nevertheless, we serve a God that specializes in removing obstacles and revealing the plan already prepared for us since the beginning of time. John 1:13 says, *"We were born, not of blood nor of the will of the flesh nor of the will of man, but of God."* Each person was uniquely created by God to carry out a specific role in life. That intended purpose is to be thoroughly connected to God in order to establish a course of divine direction. Unless we seek after God and allow Him to speak into our lives, we will never truly accomplish our journey or see the divine plans God has for us. Therefore, in order for mankind to achieve a genuine sense of purpose in life, we must give God the first portion of our heart, and we must relentlessly follow the path that is strategically designed by God for our future.

> *Therefore, brothers, be all the more diligent to confirm your calling and election, for if you practice these qualities you will never fall.* (2 Peter 1:10)

> *Declaring the end from the beginning, And from ancient times things which have not been done, Saying, "My purpose will be established, And I will accomplish all My good pleasure."* (Isaiah 46:10)

> *I press on toward the goal for the prize of the upward call of God in Christ Jesus.* (Philippians 3:14)

There is more to life than meets the eye. Allow God to do His perfect work in your life—through you, with you, and for you. God takes pleasure in revealing the parameters of your calling.

Without a Vision, People Perish

For unbelievers, accepting and receiving the counsel of God will open up numerous opportunities to discover God-given identity. But even for those of us who already honor God by relentlessly dedicating ourselves to church attendance, there is still a bigger picture. Of course our intentions are never to offend God, but many of our churches are not operating at their fullest potential. There is a considerable need for us as a church to develop into a cohesive unit reaching out to others, not only to preserve ourselves, but also to fulfill the Great Commission Jesus has urged us to establish (Matthew 28:16-20). Searching for unbelievers and helping them to be delivered from a dark, dreary world is a huge part of our journey. This mission is, of course, at the very heart of God. After all, we first knew God because He chose to know us.

In addition, spiritual maturity and the fullness of Christ are also the core of our mission. This is incorporated with spiritual growth and development—earnestly keeping ourselves purified before the Lord. As a result of these efforts, God's people can then be not only more functional in the church, but also more effective in reaching out to those outside of the church setting. If people are dying in their sins every day, why are we remaining idle and failing to reach them? And if we are not mature enough as a church, how can we then nurture new believers? So either way, one of the biggest issues we are dealing with here is maturity. As God's people, we must wholeheartedly pursue what God desires of us in order to lay the foundation of God's movement. The Bible says God is preparing an *expected end* for you (Jeremiah 29:11). The point is that God has a role for you to fill within the Body of Christ. You see, serving God is not only about attending church functions; it's about functioning in and being willing to apply yourself to the role God has ordained for you. So the questions are as follows:

1) Who are you really purposed to be?
2) Do you know what your calling is for the Lord?
3) Have you been Spirit-filled?
4) Are you sure that God has revealed to you how you are to function in the church?
5) Do you seek to pursue what God desires more than your own desires?
6) How have you taken steps to become spiritually mature and to attain the fullness of Christ?

It is paramount as a church that we pursue the plans of God. By doing so, we ascertain that we are exactly where God purposed us to be, as we *"become **mature**, attaining to the **whole measure** of the **fullness of Christ**"* (Ephesians 4:13). Be inspired to be a part of the church in order to assist in the building of God's house, which is His heart. When members of the Body of Christ still do not know what they are called to do or where their purpose for God flows, our churches will not grow into the healthy and mature congregations God intended them to be. The bottom line is that if our churches do not move out of their sense of complacency, or "sleep," they will not fulfill their assigned destinies. The ideal paradigm is to be genuinely and actively seeking after what God created us for, rather than what we have created for ourselves.

If we adhere to God's heart, the move of God will flourish in our lives and in our churches like never before. God wants revival in the churches. He wants to pour out His Spirit and saturate His churches with His presence. But we must be willing to make sacrifices, be obedient, and also step outside of our comfort zone. So I challenge you today to make sure that you, as a member of your church, can identify what you are purposed to do to demonstrate your sincerity for God. When you are face to face with your creator, will God say that you have done all He called you to do? Will God be able to say that your heart was focused on His agenda instead of your own? Be sure. Nothing is more fulfilling than knowing the character of God and how we fit into His flawless agenda.

Chapter 3

OUR CHARACTER

We live in an undeniably dark and disturbed world. Our society can be extremely troubling. The enemy Satan is deviously working throughout the earth to bring chaos to all people. His works are being seen in the spirit realm and ultimately manifested in the natural. Within our social order, we have witnessed that respecting elders has ceased. Simultaneously, the value of life is diminishing. Cursing in front of children is now being accepted. Walking the streets half naked is a style. Hate is increasingly becoming a normality. Humiliating and calling people disgraceful names is welcomed. Corruption is shockingly protected. To make things worse, hiding under denial and defiance is a new movement.

Isaiah 5:20-21 says, *"Woe to those who call **evil good** and **good evil**, who put **darkness for light** and **light for darkness**, who put **bitter for sweet** and **sweet for bitter**. Woe to those who are **wise in their own eyes and clever in their own sight.**"* It is easy to think we are right all the time. But if we do not seek God for counsel, we are deceived. Instead, we must identify with the problems of life in a way that honors God. In fact, by keeping Him first and making sure that we consider Him in every portion of our lives, our behaviors and actions will be justified. That means ensuring we avoid habitual distractions and hindrances that aid in the deterioration of unity between people. In addition, it is extremely important for us to allow God to lead us instead of relying on our own ideas. Communicating with God to ascertain whether or not we are emulating His character is a primary gesture of worship to a holy and righteous God. Character is what defines us...character is essential for the well-being of any individual and those around him/her. How we behave, how we treat others, and how we live determines how we view God for our lives. Salvation is indicative of our **behaviors and actions**. What we **speak** with **our mouths**, what we **look at** with **our eyes**, what we **entertain** in **our minds**, what we **receive** into **our hearts**, and what we **listen to** with **our ears** matters to God. The Lord wants more than anything for us all to **remain undefiled** and to **refrain** from the vanities of this world.

Honoring God also means to defend everything that concerns Him, and to pronounce His glory and absolute authority over mankind. Any efforts to discredit Almighty God should be immediately denounced. All things that contend against His will should be avoided. Distorted character and walking in the flesh have extreme consequences. If we do not honor God and His ways, He has a way of bringing us to our knees—forcing us into a corner so that we acknowledge Him. The success of our civilization is contingent upon how we submit our lives to God and how we reverence Him. In the past, societies who turned their backs on God and who were not legitimately obedient toward Him were held in some sort of **bondage** for their **actions.** For example, over and over again the people of Israel throughout biblical history defied God's way of life (Isaiah 24:1-23, NIV). Kings have displayed defiant behavior in the face of God's instructions (1 Samuel 13:1-15:33, NIV). As a result, punishment and misfortune often followed.

1) Are we genuinely sincere about things that concern God?
2) How do we treat others, and how do we legitimately view God?
3) Have we honestly sought to please God and not ourselves?

Self-reflection is paramount. Will we adhere to the will of God? And do our lips correlate with what our hearts demonstrate? Matthew 15:8-9 says, *"These people honor me with **their lips,** but **their hearts are far from Me**. They worship me in vain; their teachings are merely human* *rules."* Therefore, deciding how we will conduct ourselves in society is essential. Luke 6:45 says, *"A good person out of the good treasure of his heart brings forth good; and an evil person out of the evil treasure of his heart brings forth evil. What you say flows from what is in your heart." In addition,* Matthew 5:8 tells us, *"Blessed are the pure in heart, for they shall see God."* Let us honor God and make certain our godly stance is sure, being led of God in our behaviors and actions in the midst of all circumstances.

> *To the pure, all things are pure, but to the defiled and unbelieving, nothing is pure; but both their minds and their consciences are defiled. They profess to know God, but they deny Him by their works. They are detestable, disobedient, **unfit** for any good work.* (Titus 1:15-16)

It is not a matter of being perfect, but of **genuinely** doing our best to achieve that perfection. We should identify with what pleases God, pursue those things that pertain to Him, yield to emulate His unwavering character, and refrain from the character of this world. For all of us to emulate the character of God and to support what is at the center of His heart is paramount. Let's be sincere. This world cannot effectively direct us nor can it save us. The character of God is what enables us to effectively rebuild and establish a productive atmosphere for our society today. Refrain from the indecency of this world. Character can make us or break us and will often determine our destination.

Denouncing Idols

If we are not careful about improving our character, we contend against the authority of God. In fact, anything that takes the place of God is considered an idol, whether it be our own desires or desires for another person above God. Similarly, material belongings can be considered an idol in the eyes of God. Idols are anything that will draw us away from God as His ordinances are ignored. The book of Exodus (Chapters 31-32) is where Moses met with God on Mount Sanai. It is a passage that clearly illustrates how idols can prevent people from drawing near to the purposes of God.

When the people saw that Moses was so long in coming down from the mountain, they gathered around Aaron and said, "Come, make us gods who will go before us. As for this fellow Moses who brought us up out of Egypt, we don't know what has happened to him."

Aaron answered them, "Take off the gold earrings that your wives, your sons and your daughters are wearing, and bring them to me." So all the people took off their earrings and brought them to Aaron. He took what they handed him and made it into an idol cast in the shape of a calf, fashioning it with a tool. Then they said, "These are your gods, Israel, who brought you up out of Egypt."

When Aaron saw this, he built an altar in front of the calf and announced, "Tomorrow there will be a festival to the LORD." So the next day the people rose early and sacrificed burnt offerings and presented fellowship offerings. Afterward they sat down to eat and drink and got up to indulge in revelry.

Then the LORD said to Moses, "Go down, because your people, whom you brought up out of Egypt, have become corrupt. They have been quick to turn away from what I commanded them and have made themselves an idol cast in the shape of a calf. They have bowed down to it and sacrificed to it and have said, these are your gods, Israel, who brought you up out of Egypt." (Exodus 32:1-8)

As we read on, we see that both God and Moses were extremely angry with the people of God for worshipping the golden calf as a god, rather than submitting their honor to the Lord as they had promised. The golden calf was a display of wealth and an object of worship. In some cases, people can be viewed as idols. For instance, celebrities and superstars are considered idols, as they are greatly admired and loved by the world. They are also often symbols of wealth. And if we are not careful, we can be admiring something or someone more than we should. Idols are things that take up our time, produce awe in μs, and may even cause us to lust. Everything in this world involves satisfying one's flesh, pride, and greed. Jesus Himself was also tempted of the flesh, pride, and greed when He was fasting in the wilderness.

Then Jesus was led by the Spirit into the wilderness to be tempted by the devil. After fasting forty days and forty nights, he was hungry. The tempter came to him and said, "If you are the Son of God, tell these stones to become bread." Jesus answered, "It is written: "Man shall not live on bread alone, but on every word that comes from the mouth of God." Then the devil took him to the holy city and had him stand on the highest point of the temple. "If you are the Son of God," he said, "throw yourself down. For it is written: 'He will command his angels concerning you, and they will lift you up in their hands, so that you will not strike your foot against a stone.'" Jesus answered him, "It is also written: 'Do not put the Lord your God to the test.'" Again, the devil took him to a very high mountain and showed him all the kingdoms of the world and their splendor. "All this I will give you," he said, "if you will bow down and worship me." Jesus said to him, "Away from me, Satan! For it is written: 'Worship the Lord your God, and serve him only.'" Then the devil left him, and angels came and attended him. (Matthew 4:1-11)

The Bible also says that, *"For all that is in the world, the lust of the flesh, and the lust of the eyes, and the pride of life, is not of the Father, but is of the world"* (1 John 2:16). These are the ways in which the enemy attempts to influence us. Things we desire, or may have possession of, outside of the will of God are most likely idols. Above all, idols include anything that would direct our attention away from the plans of God for our lives.

In 1999, I had a fancy sports car. It had the shiny rims, big tires, a spoiler on the back, a noisy muffler, and the enhanced spark plugs so that the vehicle would run faster. Yet, after a divine encounter with God in the year 2000, I became a new person. I then began to seek after holiness by doing the right things and living a godly life. So nourishing my car was no longer a priority for me. I even stopped cleaning it as much.

One day during my lunch break at work, I walked outside into the parking lot and saw co-workers looking at my car. Then one of them asked me when I was going to wash it. They glared and stared at my car, as if it was so magnificent. At that moment, God let me see through His eyes that people were worshiping my car as some sort of idol. It was just like a golden calf. Furthermore, God then mentioned that many false gods exist on the earth. He showed me that there were many cars that were viewed as idols or gods in the eyes of the world. So every time I would see a vehicle that was too fancy, built-up, magnified, or even shiny, I would think about the golden calf. And when people stared so attentively at those cars, I understood the meaning of what God was trying to reveal to me.

Then, one day, God asked me, "Would a preacher or a man of God drive your car?" I then felt so much guilt because I already knew what He was showing me through my car. I tried to creatively reason with God by putting a Jesus sticker on the back window, but God said, "That's not enough—you have to represent Me and not the things of this world." So I removed the shiny rims and replaced them with the factory rims from when I initially purchased the car. Eventually, that car was replaced with another one, due to unfortunate circumstances. It was a perfect illustration of the sovereignty of God, who has control in all things for the good will of mankind.

Isaiah 51:22 speaks about God's sovereignty: *"This is what the Sovereign LORD, your God and Defender, says: 'See, I have taken the terrible cup from your hands. You will drink no more of my fury.'"* If something is hindering us from serving God more efficiently, God will remove it from our lives. The Scripture indicates that God is a jealous God, saying, *"For thou shalt worship no other god: for the LORD, whose name is Jealous, is a jealous God"* (Exodus 34:14). For this reason, we must take heed to what we exalt, magnify, or sow to the flesh. We must be mindful of our stance with the Lord to make certain we are aiming to please Him.

Sowing to the Flesh

Fundamental ways to give God pleasure usually involves spiritual matters. As we can see, a number of things can potentially distance us from Him, if we are not careful. At times, such hindrances include sowing to the flesh, which is when we tend to draw closer to possessions or world systems in place of God and His holy standards. A good analogy of sowing to the flesh can be shopping extensively. Surely, we are free to shop and find ways to please ourselves. But do we please ourselves more by satisfying our fleshly desires or do we please ourselves more by seeking God to satisfy our spiritual desires? A fleshly nature is often difficult to subdue unless we first recognize it.

Another analogy is exercising—specifically if we exercise for the wrong reasons, which can then become a form of idolatry. For instance, whenever we exercise, we must ask ourselves what our goals and intentions are in participating in this activity. The primary question is, are we seeking to achieve or sustain a healthy physical condition or are we seeking to build ourselves up in a conceited way? In other words, if we are exercising for improving the overall condition of our bodies, it is fine. On the other hand, if we are merely attempting to exalt ourselves so that other people will elevate us, exalt us, or reverence us to feed our flesh, that is identified as idolatry. Luke 14:11 says, *"For everyone who exalts himself will be humbled, and he who humbles himself will be exalted."*

One important consideration is how much time are we occupied with a particular activity. For instance, if we spend more time exercising than praying or reading God's Word, then we sow to the flesh more than the Spirit. So, if we spend more time building up the flesh, we reap more of the flesh. In contrast, if we spend more time building the spirit man, we reap more of the Spirit. Galatians 5:17 (CEV) says, *"For the desires of the flesh are against the Spirit, and the desires of the Spirit are against the flesh, for these are opposed to each other, keeping you from doing what you feel you should."* Therefore, we must recognize when we are lacking in the Spirit to avoid being taken over by our flesh. For a Christian, this is an essential aspect of spiritual warfare. If we are weak spiritually, the enemy can influence us much more easily and cause us to either sin or lure us away from God. The Bible calls for us to walk in the Spirit to avoid this. Galatians 5:16 says, *"This I say then, Walk in the Spirit, and ye shall not fulfill the lust of the flesh."*

A very familiar analogy of sowing to the flesh or practicing potential forms of idolatry is **excessive** use of cellphones. Of course, there is nothing wrong with the use of cellphones. Unfortunately, however, cellphones can become idols if we neglect the things of God, such as prayer, reading God's Word, etc., to use them instead. How much time do we spend on our cellphones? Anything that receives **more** attention than God is considered an idol and it can also sow to our flesh while gradually weakening our spiritual development. We must frequently ask ourselves how much time we actually spend on earthly activities compared to the things of God. Matthew 6:21 says, *"For where your treasure is, there will your heart be also."* Therefore, we must identify the intent of our hearts and make sure our hearts are not filled with any form of idolatry. In order to discover all of what God has planned for us, we must first seek out what He desires for us. If we utilize more of our time in spiritual guidance and direction, we will not only please God, but we will become more adept at recognizing and denouncing idols whenever they arise in our lives.

Gossip Causes Division

Denouncing strong influences that can be contrary to God's path for us is also identified as self-control. If we are not cautious enough, Satan can discover our flaws and not only lure us from God but also cause confusion between people. For the church, the Body of Christ is built on common phases of dedication and unity. Therefore, it is essential that each member work together in harmony in order to efficiently carry out God's will. However, wherever there is discord or contention, a substantial level of disunity is common. For that reason, the Bible says we are to endeavor to keep the unity of the Spirit in the bond of peace (Ephesians 4:3, NIV). Moreover, Mark 3:25 also says, *"If a house is divided against itself, that house cannot stand."*

Too often, gossip will indeed cause disunity, contention, and division among the people of God. Gossip is one of the biggest problems within churches and all over the world. It is also one of the main disruptions within the Body of Christ. In fact, if we are not watchful about guarding our minds, hearts, and mouths to combat gossip, it will not only defile us during our purification process but it can ultimately weaken the Body of Christ. The fact is that the enemy seeks to infiltrate our minds with negativity and to imbed it into our hearts, eventually causing us to speak negatively about others—instead of speaking those things that are positive or uplifting.

The enemy seeks to divide us in this way. To make things worse, gossip spreads and corrupts. So we must be vigilant in encouraging one another in efforts to build each other up and not tear each other down. At the end of the day, the enemy's ultimate goal is to influence us into speaking against one another in an effort to destroy unity between members. Speaking good things instead can be an excellent counterattack toward the enemy when being swayed to speak negatively. James 4:7 says, *"Submit yourselves therefore to God. Resist the devil, and he will flee from you."* Therefore, speaking something good about a person in such cases is an effective response to spiritual warfare.

At the same time, gossip is also considered extremely contrary to holiness. Ephesians 4:29 says: *"Let no corrupting talk come out of your mouths, but only such as is good for building up, as fits the occasion, that it may give grace to those who hear."* We must also consider being in another person's situation, or perhaps at least realizing that this life has many uncertainties for everyone. As a result, one may experience a series of events that others may never encounter. Nevertheless, we all have our own set of circumstances or troubles to resolve. For that reason, we must recognize our responsibilities as God's people by observing how we respect one another, regardless of inadequacies or circumstances. In general, whenever we notice flaws in others, it is always better to say nothing rather than something negative. Titus 3:2 admonishes us, *"Speak evil of no one, to avoid quarreling, to be gentle, and to show perfect courtesy toward all people."*

For example, several of the officers where I work were complaining about a company engineer who oversaw the electrical equipment, mentioning that he talked too much without allowing others to respond. I remember him approaching me one day and it being quite difficult to get a word in while interacting with him. However, as I began to talk about the things of God, I became aware that he knew Scripture. It was also evident that God had drawn near to him over the years. This is a prime example of why we must be careful about how we treat people who are imperfect in some way. Even though he had some flaws, no one had the right to tear him down or reject him. Moreover, in a world where many people reject the things of God, this man embraced it.

Lastly, we must recognize that gossip is not of God, and we must uplift one another rather than criticize them. Luke 6:45 says, *"A good man out of the good treasure of his heart bringeth forth that which is good; and an evil man out of the evil treasure of his heart bringeth forth that which is evil: for of the abundance of the heart his mouth speaketh."* This means if we speak good things about others, we are demonstrating goodness. If we speak negatively or evilly about others, we are demonstrating evilness. Overall, it is a reflection of our heart.

In contrast to gossip, prayer is the most productive way to manage our thoughts about others. In such instances, through prayer, we are raising up people before God and helping them along as they experience whatever problems they are facing. The fact is that if God took away His grace from any one of us, we could find ourselves in the same situation at any time. Whether we feel God is there or not, life is filled with many challenges. Therefore, it is imperative that we refrain from speaking evil about others. Let us love one another, seek unity and the bond of peace, build each other up with confidence, and cover each other in prayer—avoiding gossip at all costs.

Everywhere people are, potential gossips exist. The reality is that everyone's heart intent is not always pure or genuinely sincere. As a result, such discussions may cause a great sense of disruption between those who are involved. Gossip and backbiting divides group settings and destroys genuine friendships. Richard J. Krejcir, an author on church leadership for the Francis A. Schaeffer Institute of Church Leadership Development, indicates various problems that evolve in churches when not properly managed. According to Krejcir, within twelve years, sixty-one percent of those he surveyed left their last church because of a conflict with another member resulting from gossip or strife that would not stop, was not true, or was not properly dealt with.[2]

---

[2]   Krejcir, R.J. (2007). *Statistics On Why Churches Fail.* Schaeffer Institute of Church Leadership Development. Retrieved July 15, 2019 from http://www.truespirituality.org/.

2, 039 out of 3, 348 left due to offenses

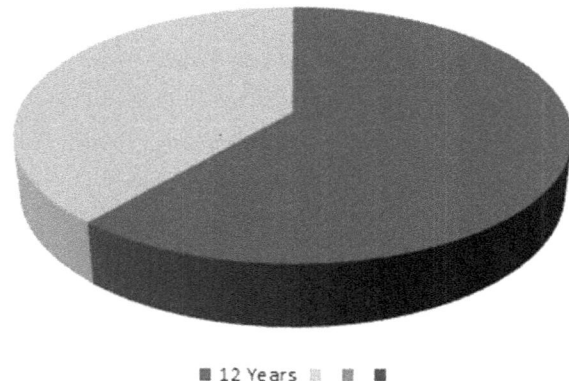

■ 12 Years ▨ ▨ ■

Therefore, as we internalize our thoughts concerning others, we must legitimately seek to build up others with positivity and sincere prayer. Instead of tearing people down with mistreatment and misplaced gestures of malice and contention, we must seek to support one another.

Tips for Avoiding Gossip

Consider these simple steps to ensure you are not involved in gossip:

1) Do not closely associate yourself with one who is a known gossip.
2) When someone starts to gossip, change the subject.
3) If you are not part of the problem or part of the solution, stay out of it.
4) If you have fallen into the bad habit of gossiping, ask God to change your heart.
5) When you have been the victim of gossip, pray for a change in the offenders' behavior and peacefully confront the parties that spread the rumor.
6) If the problem continues, focus on positive aspects of that individual rather than the negative.

7) If all else fails, inform your local church overseer for additional prayer against such contentions or to perhaps provide immediate intervention.

These methodical steps certainly can be used both inside and outside of church environments. Avoid gossip. It ruins friendships, inner groups, and even churches. Find ways to alleviate contentions without participating in episodes of gossip. Develop methods of improving cohesiveness between groups in order to yield the best results for overall objectives

Chapter 4

RESTORATION AND
HEALING FOR THE CHURCH

od expects us all to improve our relations with others and to enhance our spiritual journey. Restoration is a form of redemption or a recapturing of something that is off target. In our pursuit to become who God has purposed us to be, we find out how frail we are at times. When God's people become weakened, He finds ways to strengthen them. When they fall, He lifts them back up. After they have failed, He causes them to find the pathway to their successes. John 15:5 says, *"I am the vine; you are the branches. If you remain in ME and I in you, you will bear much fruit; apart from ME you can do nothing."* It is God who raises us up when we have lost our way of true direction, counsel, and guidance. He gives us life when we have become spiritually destitute and lifeless.

Valley of Dry Bones

The hand of the LORD was upon me, and He brought me out by the Spirit of the LORD and set me down in the middle of the valley; and it was full of bones. He caused me to pass among them round about, and behold, there were very many on

the surface of the valley; and lo, they were very dry. He said to me, "Son of man, can these bones live?" And I answered, "O Lord GOD, You know." Again He said to me, "Prophesy over these bones and say to them, 'O dry bones, hear the word of the LORD. Thus says the Lord GOD to these bones, "Behold, I will cause breath to enter you that you may come to life. I will put sinews on you, make flesh grow back on you, cover you with skin and put breath in you that you may come alive; and you will know that I am the LORD."""

So I prophesied as I was commanded; and as I prophesied, there was a noise, and behold, a rattling; and the bones came together, bone to its bone. And I looked, and behold, sinews were on them, and flesh grew and skin covered them; but there was no breath in them. Then He said to me, "Prophesy to the breath, prophesy, son of man, and say to the breath, 'Thus says the Lord GOD, "Come from the four winds, O breath, and breathe on these slain, that they come to life.""" So I prophesied as He commanded me, and the breath came into them, and they came to life and stood on their feet, an exceedingly great army.

Explanation of the Vision

Then He said to me, "Son of man, these bones are the whole house of Israel (God's people); behold, they say, 'Our bones are dried up (spiritually misguided and depleted) and our hope has perished. We are completely cut off.' Therefore prophesy and say to them, 'Thus says the Lord GOD, "Behold, I will open your graves and cause you to come up out of your graves, My people; and I will bring you into the land of Israel. Then you will know that I am

the LORD, when I have opened your graves and caused
you to come up out of your graves, My people. I will put
My Spirit within you and you will come to life, and I will
place you on your own land. Then you will know that I,
the LORD, have spoken and done it," declares the LORD.'
(Ezekiel 37:1-14)

Basically, "the breath of God" is a symbol of life in the form of God's presence. The people of God were restored and transformed into a mighty army for the Lord—spiritually renewed and restored. Well, this is essentially restoration...restoration means *to return to, to redevelop or to rebuild.* It is a clear illustration of spiritual strengthening and awareness.

The Recovery

We must determine what pleases God and recover from whatever causes the stagnation of our efforts. Let us make every year about accomplishing whatever God wants from us. God is calling some to step up into the fivefold ministry. Some are called to be helpers of support within the ministry. God is calling others to give more to the church monetarily, socially, and spiritually as part of the church. For the most part, it is a greater sense of commitment and dedication to promote the kingdom of God for His glory. Our reasonable service is to ensure that we seek to live holy lives in the sight of God; yet, it is also to do whatever God calls us to do for Him in willingness and obedience (Romans 12:21).

Isaiah 6:8 says, *"Then I heard the voice of the Lord, saying, 'Whom shall I send, and who will go for us?' Then I said, 'Here am I. Send me!'"* Just imagine if we all spent more time in prayer, more time reading the Word of God, more time witnessing to others about the glory of salvation, and more time seeking His divine direction. We would see God move in ways greater than our imagination. The way we embrace restoration is a call to deeper depths in God. This, of course, is allowing

God to overflow us with His anointing and to pour His presence upon us in a very special way.

Do not cast me away from Your presence. And do not take Your Holy Spirit from me. Restore to me the joy of Your salvation. And sustain me with a willing spirit. Cast me not away from thy presence; and take not thy holy spirit from me. Restore to me the joy of your salvation and grant me a willing spirit, to sustain me. (Psalm 51:9-12)

It is imperative that we step outside of our comfort zone and allow God to use us as He pleases—not just living life, but speaking life into our future by having faith and trusting in God concerning godly purposes. We shouldn't fall into complacency or be idle in daily life settings, or even be content in church fellowship alone. Oftentimes, God leads us to do more. Church is about being a part of "the Movement of God" in a way that could perhaps further aid God in building His church (Ephesians 4:16, NIV).

Just imagine a new member who attends church and is not yet involved in anything concerning the Body of Christ. At the same time, imagine a seasoned member who facilitates and conducts Bible studies on a regular basis. Lastly, imagine God then observing these two members and desiring more from each. Of course, God would like to fill the first member with the baptism of the Holy Ghost and begin to use that person's gifts and talents for the church. The second member may already be filled with the Holy Ghost and facilitates Bible studies regularly—yet God wants more. You see, our work is never done until we stop breathing…God has a heart to develop and release members for the Fivefold ministry, to utilize whatever spiritual gifts members have to coordinate the church, to reach out to the lost with outreach missions, and for His people to diligently seek after His presence. However, if we remain idle, get too relaxed, or linger in complacency, we will miss the movement of God. God is calling some of us to do more than what we are already doing or perhaps to yearn for a deeper sense of responsibility and accountability. Being able to forgive others and seek forgiveness in our short comings is essential. We must set our hearts on preserving others as much as ourselves. In this way, we exhibit the mercy of Jesus has for us all when we need a helping hand in the recovery process. And for many of us, Gods mercy has proven to endure.

Chapter 5

THE MERCY AND FORGIVENESS OF CHRIST

Let us look at things from a deeper perspective. The mercies of God are profound and unmatchable. When we make mistakes or have somehow fallen short, he is there to help us in the recovery process. In a world of uncertainty and confusion, there is a **life that stems beyond** the aimlessness of our lives. When we face numerous conflicts, issues, and concerns, Jesus said He is our light of hope in a dark and dreary world. *"I am the light of the world. Whoever follows me will never walk in darkness, but will have the **light of life."*** (John 8:12)

It may sometimes seem that God is not so near, but He is attentive to our needs. We need, first, only to have a dedicated heart to embrace that life and do what is right in the sight of the Lord. The Bible says, *"For everyone has sinned; we all fall short of God's glorious standard"* (Romans 3:23). Therefore, God knows the heartaches, frustration, and hidden flaws embodied within each and every one of us. Yet, as we identify our frailties, He forgives and remembers our sin no more (Hebrews 10:17).

1 Samuel 16:7 teaches us, *"For the Lord sees not as man sees; for man looks on the outward appearance, but **the Lord looketh on the heart."*** If God forgives us, we must likewise choose to forgive others. People have a tendency to point fingers at the mistakes and inconsistencies of others. To illustrate, the Scripture says that Jesus allowed a woman in her sinful condition to touch Him when He was near the northern shore of the

Sea of Galilee. He rebuked several others for their judgmental spirit and blessed her with forgiveness and favor (Luke 7:36-50).

Today, I want you to consider what He did, as difficult as it seems to think about. How in His mercy, He gave His life for us all despite our mistakes. We must also overcome the unpleasant sins of others. Because, you see, God sees them differently than how we see them. Even if people don't deserve it, let us show mercy and forgiveness to others the same way the Lord has demonstrated mercy and forgiveness for us. We must remember their sin against us no more. Likewise, we should be forgiven. Suppose you were in the same situation as the woman in Galilee? Perhaps you were desperate and needed a break from a regretful mistake? Matthew 6:15 says, *"But if you do not forgive others their sins, your Father will not forgive your sins."*

Suffering of Jesus

Regardless of how uprightly we live, we will still sometimes suffer at the hand of others around us. It does not matter how much we support or encourage others, we will still perhaps be mistreated in some way. It is equivalent to walking in the footsteps of Jesus. In fact, in order for us to understand Jesus, oftentimes we must be able to partake in His suffering and feel what He must have felt. Many times throughout my journey, I have had a taste of how Jesus must have felt in very extreme situations. It can, at times, be heart-wrenching and desolate. But one thing I can promise is that Jesus illustrates to you in those moments the intensity of what He experienced. He wants us to see what He sees and sense what He felt.

All throughout the New Testament, it says Jesus healed the sick, the lame, and the blind. He cast out demons; He raised the dead from the grave; He multiplied food for the hungry; He taught on the Scriptures (Matthew 9:35, Mark 2:9-12, John 9:6-7, Mark 3:11, John 11:38-44, John 6:1-14, John 11:38-44). And, without a doubt, I know great display of holiness had to be seen in the life of Jesus. We also realize that God allowed the enemy, Satan, to heavily influence Jewish leaders and the Roman soldiers in order to capture Him, so that the Scriptures could be fulfilled (John 18:1-12). Regardless of those unfortunate arrangements, Jesus had a divine purpose. That purpose was much greater than the hatred against Him, and His suffering was more extensive than Christians today typically encounter.

After Jewish leaders accused Him of being a troublemaker (John 18:28-38), after they beat Him (John 19:1-22), after they chose to free the murderer Barabbas instead of Him (Matthew 27:17), after they mocked Him (Matthew 27:27-31), after they spit on Him (Matthew 26:67) and yanked out His beard (Isaiah 50:6), after they whipped Him (John 19:1), after they put a crown of thorns on His head (John 19:2), and after they nailed Him cruelly to the cross (Luke 23:26-43), Jesus said in Luke 23:34, *"Father, forgive them, for they know not what they do."*

In actuality, Jesus was saying, "I forgive them because...

- they don't know that I am the Father the Son and the Holy Ghost, all in one (John 1:1-11).
- they don't know that I AM the One that created the world (John 1:1-11).
- they don't know that I AM the Alpha and the Omega (John 1:1-11).
- they don't know that I AM the creator of life and apart from ME, they can do nothing (John 1:1-11).
- they don't know that I AM their only means of peace and redemption (John 1:1-11).
- they don't know I AM the Lord Most High (John 1:1-11).
- they don't know I AM the Lord of Hosts, and there is no one else above ME (John 1:1-11).

He said, "I forgive them, because they don't know."

Our Lord Jesus knew that not only was He there on the cross for those who rejected Him, but also He would make Himself more accessible to those who would come forth and receive Him. And at times, when we diligently stand for Christ, we as followers of Jesus must live in the midst of rejection and mistreatment regardless of how difficult things seem. The only times we are urged not to be tolerant toward others is when God has specifically led us in another direction for our spiritual journey. Otherwise, we are advised to stay, endure, and partake in the sufferings the Lord has imparted to us. Matthew 5:11-12 commands, *"Blessed are you when people insult you, persecute you and falsely say all kinds of evil against you because of me. Rejoice and be glad, for your reward is great in heaven, for so they persecuted the men of God who were before you."*

First Love Scripture

The spiritual journey the Lord imparts to us is not always easy. But we must also realize that the sacrifice Jesus has shown for the world was far more extensive. In fact, we have certainly not encountered the kind of suffering Christ poured out for us. It can be a demanding mission for the average person. But there are many Christians who are not so reluctant in how they deal with issues of adversity and hardship. However, at the same time, we must ensure that we maintain the same connection we encountered with the Lord from the beginning of our salvation. The times when we could not wait to be in the Lord's presence and to obey His every word. Or perhaps times when we wanted to tell everyone about the marvelous salvation of Jesus and when we were just waiting for God to use us.

Revelation 2:3-4 says, *"You have persevered and have endured hardships for my name, and have not grown weary. Yet I hold this against you: You have forsaken the love you had at first."* One thing we must understand is that God will never force us, but He will gracefully nudge us so we can self-reflect and perhaps consider whether we are exactly where He wants us to be within the Body of Christ. We should really focus on seeking to build the house of God so that evangelism efforts can flourish and the church can be effective in a troubled world.

Healthy evangelism stems from the local church, from the inside out, to impact surrounding areas. This requires making sure our existing members are prepared to mentor newcomers when the increase comes. Minister and missionary C.T. Studd once quoted, *"The light that shines farthest shines brightest at home."*[3] In other words, if we can be demonstrations of light to the Body of Christ itself, we can then be lights to a dark world. However, our shining begins at home. We should be saying, "God, use me; I am willing to be used for Your glory's sake." Some of us feel inadequate or afraid to step up into certain commitments. However, Jeremiah 32:27 says, *"I am the LORD, the God of all mankind. Is anything too hard for me?"* Essentially, this means if God calls us to do something, He will work through us to make it happen. We need only to avoid distractions. There is a deeper way in God if we take only a few more steps higher to reach Him. It is the essence of holiness in an unholy world of unruliness and mischief.

---

[3]   Studd, C.T. (2011). *Learning the Practices of Ministry*, Church of God School of Ministry. Cleveland: Tennessee.

Chapter 6

HOLINESS FOR GOD'S PEOPLE

irst of all, it is my prayer that each person reading this message has ears to hear what the Spirit of the Lord is saying to them and that, collectively, we will be a church without spot or wrinkle. *"That he might present it to himself a glorious church, not having spot, or wrinkle, or any such thing; but that it should be holy and without blemish."* (Ephesians 5:27) Holiness is a process of keen self-reflection. What we do inside and outside of formal church functions defines who we really are in relation to character and spiritual maturity. We are not perfect, but we should always strive to be for the sake of righteousness. God wants to refine us, purify us, and stretch us further into His path of holiness. Let us view this subject from a different angle.

In the Bible, Babylon and Egypt both represented the enemy. The captivity of Israel by Egypt represented the bondage of God's people (Exodus 6:6). In this day and time, captivity can also represent spiritual captivity that hinders the spiritual growth or progress of God's people. The enemy Satan oppresses God's people in many forms—even in hidden forms. For instance, if we do not abstain from all appearances of evil (1 Thessalonians 5:22), the enemy will infiltrate or gain advantage over our purification processes. In order to be free from all forms of captivity and to progress, we must reverence God "in all things." More to the point, we must reject or avoid anything that intermingles with a worldly lifestyle. 1 Corinthians 10:31 says, *"Whether you eat or drink, or whatever you do, do all to the glory of God."*

What fellowship does light have with darkness (2 Corinthians 6:14)? Are there guidelines or standards for holiness? Yes, Isaiah 6:3 says so: *"Holy, holy, holy is the LORD of hosts; the whole earth is full of his glory!"* In addition, 1 Peter 1:16 says, *"For it is written, be ye holy for I am holy."* At all times, we must be watchful of what we do, what we look at with our eyes, what we embrace in our hearts, what we welcome into our minds, what we choose to listen to with our ears, and what we say out of our mouths. When this purification process is obtained by applying these disciplines, it leads to holiness. Romans 12:2 says, *"And do not be conformed to this world, but be transformed by the renewing of your mind, so that you may prove what the will of God is, that which is good and acceptable and perfect (holy)."* Galatians 5:16 says, *"This I say then, Walk in the Spirit, and ye shall not fulfill the lust of the flesh."*

Yet, as we mentioned earlier, the Bible says people will sometimes hear what they want to hear and do what they want to do. In other words, they only do what pleases them, instead of what is pleasing to the Lord. 2 Timothy 4:3 says, *"For the time will come when people will not put up with sound doctrine. Instead, to suit their own desires, they will gather around them a great number of teachers to say what their itching ears want to hear."* This is certainly a huge problem for those who consider themselves Christians, but then refuse to live godly as God intended. Matthew 15:8 even says, *"These people honor me with their lips, but their hearts are far from me."* The Bible further indicates that some people are double-minded (James 1:8). An unteachable spirit lacks humility and ultimately obstructs a consecrated lifestyle. In fact, the lack of a solid prayer life or maybe even the refusal to adhere to the Scriptures can definitely prevent spiritual growth. And to adhere does not mean to live holy one day and live carnally the next. Holiness is a way of life and a standard of living for God's people—every day. If not, then serving God apart from that becomes a ritual. We cannot embrace the things of the world and embrace God at the same time. *"No one can serve two masters—being devoted to one, you despise the other"* (Matthew 6:24).

Revelation 3:16 also says, *"So, because you are lukewarm, and neither hot nor cold, I will spit you out of my mouth."*

We must be careful not to combine our holy place of worship with secular lifestyle practices. Our place of worship is holy ground and we are called to be a holy people. We cannot turn God on and off like a switch when we want to. Our walk is continuous—even through our music. Let us examine ourselves to see if we give God pleasure even in the music we embrace. Do we give God honor through secular music? Do we sense God's presence while listening to secular music or praise and worship music? In which way do we honor God? Are we more concerned with pleasing ourselves with the secular music we embrace or pleasing God? Have we completely turned away from worldly desires? Titus 2:12 says, *"And we are instructed to deny ungodliness and worldly desires and to live sensibly, righteously and godly in the present age."*

Can you imagine the people of Israel listening and dancing to pagan music instead of music that uplifted God? I can picture that during their rebellious stage. This most likely occurred in Exodus 20:1-7, where they gave allegiance to false gods and, of course, God was not pleased, bringing them eventually into captivity because of their unfaithfulness. In the book of Genesis, God also told the man named Lot to gather up his family and leave the city of Sodom and Gomorrah as a result of defilement in the land. Lot's wife Ado (Edith) was instructed not to look back at her past (Genesis 19:15-26). Yet, she looked back upon her old life and longed for what did not please God. In doing that, she refused to obey what God desired and the Bible says she was turned into a pillar of salt due to her disobedience. If we look back upon our secular (worldly) music with longing, we are no different than Lot's wife. You see, we are not judged by our past; we are only judged by our past when we return to our past—the part of the past that does not please God nor uplift His kingdom.

Let us not look back at something that does not honor God and is part of the world. The truth is that God is not pleased with His children accepting secular music outside of formal church settings. The Lord loves you, but there is a better place—a higher place—than this. Music matters. Matthew 7:14 says, *"Because strait is the gate, and narrow is the way, which leadeth unto life, and few there be that find it."*

Discipleship

The Lord has fashioned us in a way that we retain our own free-will by assuming our minds and hearts - ultimately determining our own path. That's one reason the scripture says, *"Above all, guard the heart, for out of it are the issues of life"* (Proverbs, 4:23). There are many distractions. However, God has faithfully led mankind towards the narrow way of eternal life through the hope and redemption of salvation shed upon the cross through Jesus Christ - regardless of the interferences and adversities of this world. Yet, mankind, for thousands and thousands of years has sought after everything except God's mind and God's heart. Instead they have pursued their own selfish desires and pleasure. There is an enormous urge for a path of discipline for God's people. People who are God-driven – a remnant, an army that will preserve God's principles. This is the embodiment of discipleship.

Discipleship and discipline are one... And your aim towards God's heart depends on it... Being a ***disciple is being set apart for God's use***. Remaining **consecrated** and seeking out our **preparation** is paramount. That preparation is orchestrated not primarily by the help of men, but first and foremost by the hand of God. It is a choosing of God's purposeful agenda for one's life. The Bible makes plain that Jesus Himself chose His disciples (Luke 5:1-11) based on what He saw in them and not based on what they saw within themselves. As Jesus walked beside the Sea of Galilee, he saw two brothers, named Peter and his brother Andrew. They were fisherman and were casting a net into the lake. "Come, follow me," Jesus said, "and I will make you fishers of men." Immediately, they left their nets and followed him. According to Matthew, Jesus called his twelve disciples to him and gave them authority to drive out impure spirits and to heal every disease and sickness. He appointed the twelve of them that they might adhere to his teachings and that he might send them out to preach with the authority to drive out demons.

In fact, before we ever searched within ourselves, God has already made a determination concerning us. He has created each and every one of us for a godly purpose. Without a doubt, life is much bigger than us. It involves the hand of God speaking into our very existence as we attempt to navigate through many unwarranted obstacles. A true follower of Christ does not follow after the foolish things of the world. But a fulfilled life is contingent upon us observing and obeying the higher call. In order to be a disciple, one must consider a momentous path in the direction that emulates Jesus' works of service toward all mankind. It is a glorious endeavor that only Jesus can thoroughly lead us into. It can be demanding and extremely sacrificial, yet rewarding. John 15:8 says, *"By this My Father is glorified, that you bear much fruit and so prove to be My disciples."* God is willing to lead us to a deeper place through Him beyond our natural abilities, gifts, and talents. There is a spiritual realm at play that only God Himself can unfold. And I will be the first one to tell you that I can do nothing without the hand of God. In fact, if it were not for the empowerment of the Lord, I would not have the boldness to minister in front of church congregations. The Bible says, *"Those who cleanse themselves will be instruments for special purposes, made holy, useful to the master and prepared to do any good work"* (2 Tim. 2:21).

Of course we all have our flaws. But God has a strategic method for purging and transforming us into what He purposes for us. Our existence is founded on preserving God's presence around us and maintaining divine alignment. Sometimes in order to position ourselves properly, God must show us where He has been in order to take us in the Spirit where He is. And before we can lead, we must first go through testing and learn to serve others. A disciple is restrained in humility. A disciple is willing to make sacrifices, remain obedient, endure hardship, and preserve morality. Anyone can mention God, but will we do what

He says? In fact, when dying to self, it does not mean to justify our continuous lifestyle without His counsel. It means that we must preserve God's standards above our own. God wants spiritual growth in the church. He wants to use those who are willing to be used. God wants to manifest the gifts of the Holy Spirit. Right now as we

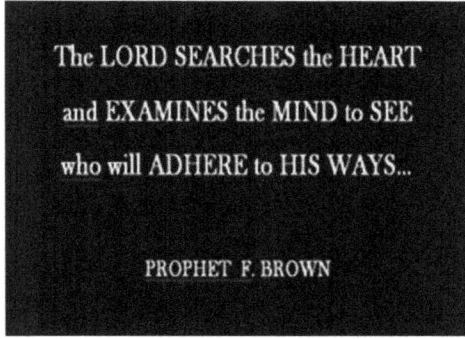

The LORD SEARCHES the HEART and EXAMINES the MIND to SEE who will ADHERE to HIS WAYS...

PROPHET F. BROWN

speak He's building disciples. He wants to birth something out of you. But the issues of life can pull us into various directions if we let it. For some, they find themselves in a vicious cycle of unfulfillment and discontentment. However, our lives were never meant to remain lost, uncertain or complacent. God has purposed us for more than reaching for him in a time of despair. God has always and will always desire His creation closely connected without worldy distraction and ungodly temptations. Jesus said, *"Whoever wants to be My disciples must deny themselves and take up their cross daily and follow Me"* (Luke 9:23).

Dying to self does not mean to justify ongoing lifestyles of sin or slothfulness. It means to preserve God's standards over your own... Dying to self wisely means we don't matter as much as God does. Unquestionably, being purged by God's hand is not usually comfortable. In essence, God sees the deficiencies or impurities in us and finds ways to drive them out. In addition, if we are weak in one area of perspective, He enlightens us with harsh refinement. I been there and sometimes I still do go there - it hurts. But in it, God shows me exactly what He went through. Being hated for little or no cause, envied, slandered, misunderstood, competed against, rejected, backbitten, and neglected. At the same time, in these moments He reveals the art of humility. When our heart is broken and settles in humility it is filled with attentiveness and submission. We tend to listen more when we are in dire situations. This is because we self-reflect in these moments and will often acknowledge God more keenly.

Oftentimes we will even hear God's voice of direction and counsel more clearly. And if we allow God's perfect process, He shapes, molds, and sculptures us into the man or woman of God He purposed us to be. But it is never meant for us to go through life alone. In the midst of refinement, we commune with God by seeing what He sees. And without reservation, He resides with us every step of the way. We all have seen and discovered our frailty at some time or another. But one thing we must keep in mind is that life belongs to God and His path is divinely placed upon us to pursue. And if God's path is at the forefront of our mortality, then we must sensibly consider His guidelines for us to follow. It will take some effort. It may be difficult. It may even be extremely sacrificial. But we must endure by pursuing the purification process God has allocated for us.

The Bible says, *"Examine yourselves, to see whether you are in the faith. Test yourselves."* (2 Corinthians 13:5). If we follow Him in one area of scripture, but neglect other areas we are incomplete in maturity. We must pursue spiritual maturity. It is the divine destination of our journey. We must make sure the Lord is at the first portion of our hearts and He will solidify our purpose. It can literally save our lives.

> Matthew 16:25 says, *"For whoever wants to save their life will lose it, but whoever loses their life for Me will find it."*

> Luke 14:27 further says, *"And whoever does not carry their cross and follow me cannot be my disciple."*

I would like to make a declaration again that anyone can mention God. But will you do what He says?... In everything you do, make sure it honors God. If the things you do, think about look at, say, listen to does not lift up God, then don't do it. As my mentor used to say, "Whenever in doubt, don't do it." We must not be selective with God's word. None of it returns void unto Him.

Psalms 119:9 says, *"How can a young person stay on the path of purity? By living according to Your word."*

John 8:31-32 further says, *"If you abide in my word, you are truly My disciples, and you will know the **truth**, and the **truth** will set you **free**."*

And we are also called to go out into the world as disciples to help unbelievers discover that truth. Matthew 28:19 says, *"Therefore go and make disciples of all nations, baptizing them in the name of the Father and of the Son and of the Holy Spirit, and teaching them to obey everything I have commanded you. And surely I am with you always, to the very end of the age.'*

God is looking for disciples who will lead at the front, stand in the gap if needed, and maintain a firm foundation to stand upon. He has masterfully made plain the significance of His counsel and the stability of His flawless foundation. That foundation consists of those who will uphold the Gospel of Jesus within the parameters of sound doctrine. It also entails preserving whatever pleases Him and determining what is needed to help strengthen His people. But in order to strengthen others we must first strengthen ourselves. It is a much deeper journey than what we can accomplish on our own. God's Word is infallible, directional, and imparts knowledge. For that reason, a good foundation for a path of discipleship is comprised of purity and abiding by the scriptures.

"For no man *can lay a FOUNDATION other than the one which is laid, which is JESUS CHRIST"* (1 Corinthians 3:11).

A true follower of Christ does not follow the profane nor the ungodly. Instead, they discover and pursue a deeper sense of alignment with the things of God. Disciples draw near enough to hear God's voice to accomplish whatever He has planned.

Listening for God's Voice

As we commune with Jesus, we must know how to hear His voice, not to always depend on others for a word from God, but to hear from God for ourselves. If we don't, we will not mature and develop into good listeners who will benefit from God's sense of direction and warning. In addition, the fact is that church leaders will not always be available to counsel their members every minute of the day. Above all, it's primarily about that connection with God over mankind. So we must be able to identify with God's voice and depend on that particular instruction at any moment that it is given. Mankind has many flaws, but the glory of the Lord never fails. Nevertheless, if you acknowledge God and consider His ways, then you are worthy to hear His voice. God speaks in a variety of ways. We often see Him speak through the Word of God. At times, He speaks through other people. Sometimes He shows us signs or warnings. Many people have dreams and some even encounter visions. But the most important thing that most of us need to be able to do is hear God's voice. John 10:27 says, *"My sheep listen to **My Voice**; I know them, and they **Follow Me**."*

God speaks...We must listen. The direction of your life is contingent upon how keenly you listen for God's voice. Without a doubt, prayer is our divine communication with God and an ideal way of hearing His voice. However, prayer is ***not*** meant to just speak and not listen. In the same way that we communicate with others around us by listening, we should also apply the art of listening with God. After we have poured out our hearts to the Lord, be careful not to just walk away. God also has a message for us. God's duty is to speak—our duty is to hear. If you are willing to listen, He will be willing to speak. God is always speaking. Make sure you are always listening. However, don't wait until your prayer is over to listen for God's voice. Listen while sharing your prayer. If not, at least be sure to listen at the very end, as God is usually attempting to communicate with us while we pray. It's sort of like the Prophet Samuel when he was a young boy.

Isaiah 6:8 says, *"Then I heard the voice of the LORD, saying, "Whom shall I send, and who will go for us?" Then I said, "Here am I. Send me!"*

Once you know what it is like to hear God's voice, you should always search for it. Jeremiah 33:3 says, *"**Call to Me** And I will **Answer You** and tell you great and unsearchable things you do not know."* In Revelations 3:20, Jesus tells us, *"**Here I Am!** I stand at the door and knock. If anyone hears **My Voice** and opens the door, I will come in and eat with that person, and they with **Me.**"* The more time we spend with God, the more we will be able to recognize and perceive His voice. When God speaks, you will feel a strong impression and hear a still, small voice—followed by His presence being felt.

Chapter 7

BE WATCHFUL & PRAY

Hosea 4:6 says, *"My people are destroyed for the lack of knowledge."*

➢ We lack knowledge about what we do not know.
➢ We lack knowledge about what we are not aware of.
➢ We lack knowledge about what we do not perceive.

In the year 2002, God gave me a revelation concerning the strongholds of darkness. They are often sent or distributed into the earth by small groupings of demonic forces out to the world and to churches. Their mission is to learn about us and discover our faults and weaknesses so they can capitalize on them. Once they learn our weaknesses, they then attempt to infiltrate our minds with negative or evil thoughts. If we entertain those thoughts, we receive that defilement into our hearts. The third phase is if we embrace evil thoughts into our minds and hearts, we become contrary to the Spirit of God or to the move of God. In fact, we know that the Scriptures mention that *"we do not wrestle with flesh and blood, but against principalities, against powers, against the rulers of the darkness of this world, against spiritual wickedness in high places"* (Ephesians 6:12).

Therefore, these forces contend with the will of God by attempting to divide us—so we will not function properly as the Body of Christ. If they are successful in infiltrating our minds, then divisions between people or members may occur. The manifestations of these occurrences involve all kinds of conflicts: episodes of envying, misjudging, and speaking evil of one another, etc. In fact, these forces may even attempt to influence us to think too highly of ourselves instead of remaining humble. Additional contentions include gossip and backbiting, which are some of the biggest problems in churches all over the world. Without discipline or holiness within those assembled, the church will not be as effective. In other words, the church will be unable to operate at the level of holiness God desires. As a result, God's divine presence can be thwarted or limited. Indeed, we must be mindful of these evil forces that come against us and the things of God. The demonic forces' primary goal is to hinder sinners and believers from serving God effectively. Undeniably, we are in a battle between good and evil. Jesus is identified as the symbol of goodness, while Satan is the symbol of evil. Jesus saves lives, but in contrast, John 10:10 says that Satan comes only to steal, kill, and destroy.

Jesus, when in the Garden of Gethsemane, knew that evil influences and satanic distractions existed when He said in Mark 14:38, *"Be watchful and pray that you may not enter into temptation. The spirit indeed is willing, but the flesh is weak."* Therefore, our lives consist of a spiritual battle. As the Scriptures mention, spiritual warfare is real, and non-physical forces are at work to prevent God's people from achieving their purposes upon the earth. 2 Corinthians 10:4-5 says, *"For the weapons of warfare are not carnal (it's not natural, it's spiritual). But mighty through God for the pulling down of strongholds, casting down things that are contrary to God and everything that exalts itself against the knowledge of God, bringing every thought into captivity to the obedience of Christ.* How many people realize we are in a continuous battle between good and evil? The fact is that the moment you were born, Satan wanted to destroy you...therefore, a Christian's life is indeed filled with warfare. Unless we view life that way and learn techniques for overcoming our adversary, we will live defeated lives. But God has divinely positioned us for victory. Malachi 4:3 says, *"And you shall tread down the wicked;*

for they shall be ashes under the soles of your feet in the day that I shall do this, saith the Lord of hosts."

Our weapons of warfare contribute greatly to our successes in combatting the enemy. The enemy attempts to influence us through our senses. For that reason, we must be mindful of our behaviors and actions to solidify our allegiance to the Lord.

The Mind

The enemy seeks to infiltrate our minds and hearts to produce anything contrary to the will of God. Therefore, we must guard ourselves from these attacks. In fact, the most extensive strategy the enemy uses to hinder people from serving God is through the mind and the heart. You see, when evil thoughts enter our minds, we must consider that Satan is tempting us or trying to influence us in some way. 2 Corinthians 10:5 says, *"Bringing **every thought** into captivity to the obedience of Christ,"* which means to submit to the will of God through our minds. In other words, our battle against the enemy begins with walking in the spirit and guarding the mind. Romans 12:2 says, *"Do not be conformed to this world, but be transformed by the **renewal of your mind**, that by testing you may discern the will of God, what is good and acceptable and perfect."*

What do you daydream about? What is your primary goal in life? Do you have any underlying desires to achieve? What do you think about most of the time? Whatever you answered, your mind and heart is there also. And if our minds do not have God in them, then we probably do not genuinely have God in our hearts. This means we must remain watchful by acknowledging our thought patterns, as we prevent ourselves from undesired defilement.

Guard the mind.

The Heart

It is imperative that we prevent evil or ungodly thoughts from entering into the heart. How we react to those thoughts determines what we will ultimately receive into our hearts. Psalm 51:10 says, *"Create in me a **clean heart**, O God; and renew a **right spirit** within me."* Proverbs 4:23 says, *"Above all else, **guard your heart**, for out of it are the issues of life."*

What we focus on is what we become. In other words, the heart and the mind determine what we will pursue and how we will seek to live our lives. If we desire something, our hearts and minds will be included. Psalm 119:10-11 says, *"I seek you with **all my heart**; do not let me stray from your commandments. I have hidden your word **in my heart** that I might not sin against you."* For that reason, it is imperative that we monitor thoughts that enter into the mind and filter into the heart every day. Luke 6:45 says: *"The good person out of the good treasure of his heart produces good, and the evil person out of the evil treasure produces evil, for out of the abundance of the heart his mouth speaks."*

What we think in our minds and embrace in our hearts is evidenced by how we conduct ourselves and how we interact within society. Our hearts and minds exhibit what we value in life. If our hearts and minds are set on a particular goal, we will pursue it. Wherever our hearts and minds are focused, we follow.

Genesis 6:5 also says, *"The Lord saw that the wickedness of man was great in the earth, and that every intention of the thoughts of his heart was only evil continually."* God does, and has always, sought for our hearts and minds to desire Him. Putting God first in our hearts consists of being mindful of everything that interferes with our divine connection to His will.

Guard the heart.

The Eyes

As you know, the eyes are what we use to take in details or to acquire specific information from our environment. For that reason, it is essential for us to be watchful over what we observe with our eyes. Another spiritual attack from the enemy is through the eyes when we see things that are contrary to God's will. Many things we see and embrace with our eyes, our minds, and our hearts can corrupt us if we entertain them. It is always best to guard, avoid, and turn away from these attacks by the enemy. 1 John 2:15-17 says, *"For all that is in the world is the **lust of the flesh**, the **lust of the eyes**, and the pride of life."*

This ultimately means that the world operates in a way that opposes God's will. It is a lifestyle that focuses on the concepts of lust, pride, greed, and boastfulness. Galatians 5:17 says, *"For the flesh wars against the spirit, and the spirit against the flesh: and these are contrary the one to the other: so that ye cannot do the things that ye would."* Therefore, we must be mindful of the constant battle for our eyes in order to assure that we are in God's will, being attentive and aware enough to entertain what is godly and avoiding all appearances of evil (1 Thessalonians 5:22).

Guard the eyes.

The Mouth

Guarding the mouth is equally important. We must guard the mouth from evil speaking, foolish conversation, and confusion. Psalm 34:13 says, *"Keep your tongue from evil and **your lips from speaking lies.** Set a guard O Lord over my mouth: keep watch over the door of my lips."* Ephesians 4:29 commands, *"Let **no corrupting talk come out of your mouths**, but only such as is good for building up, as fits the occasion, that it may give grace to those who hear."*

A bitter or unruly tongue can cause many problems between people, as well as among groups and in social environments. As a result, people are divided, friends are lost, and a great lack of unity is displayed. Titus

3:2 says, *"Speak evil of no one, to avoid quarreling, to be gentle, and to show perfect courtesy toward all people."* Proverbs 4:24 tells us, *"If anyone thinks he is religious and does not bridle his tongue this person's religion is worthless."*

We are in a society where people are being taught to speak their minds and say whatever they want to say. However, in order for a society to flourish, we must first be courteous to one another. Courtesy includes being careful what we say to one another and about one another, making sure that what is spoken is morally sound in the sight of God.

Guard the mouth.

The Ears

In reference to guarding the ears, it is necessary to be mindful of what we entertain with our ears for the sake of sanctity—being consecrated and sanctified through the Lord Jesus Christ. Romans 12:1 says, *"It is our duty to present our bodies as a living sacrifice, HOLY and ACCEPTABLE unto God, which is our reasonable service."*

How many of you have heard someone curse around you? Or perhaps someone gossips about another? Of course, sometimes we cannot control our environment. For instance, while at work, we might not able to prevent ourselves from hearing profanity or secular music. However, if we do have a way of escape, then we should take it. Many secular music artists are proven to be Satan worshippers. True crime artifacts collector Jessika M. Thomas mentions that many famous individuals have surprising connections to LaVey and the Church of Satan.[4] Similar to those findings, former culture editor, music critic, columnist and interviewer Martin Chilton also indicates that open and hidden satanic content is often placed within the musical lyrics of many

---

[4] Thomas, J.M. (2019). *Famous People You Didn't Know Had Connections To Satanism*. The Ranker. Retrieved November 7, 2019 from https://www.ranker.com/list/famous-satanists/jessika-gilbert.

celebrities as they perform for their audiences.[5] According to Spiritual Developer and Counselor David Arkyn, many forces are working in this world to keep people asleep.[6] His recent interest has been researching the psychological tactics and techniques used to limit people's spiritual potential.

Many secular music artists perform songs concerning Satan and also promote satanic symbolisms in their videos. The familiar saying "Do as you will" is promoted rather than what God wants. These visual representations of defiance are identified as "the one eye" or the "triangle" and "two horns," which are all symbols of Satan.[7] Moreover, those involved in such projects are often individuals we would never suspect of participating in satanic rituals. Avoiding these encounters by guarding the eyes and ears can ultimately enhance one's purification process.

James 4:4 says, *"Therefore whoever wishes to be a friend of the world makes himself an **enemy of God**."* Therefore, those who are receptive and teachable will seek to possess a spiritual life and continue to grow toward the things of God: ***godly concerns, godly matters, godly conversation.*** Romans 12:12 commands us, *"And do not be conformed to this world, but be **transformed** by the **renewing of your mind**, so that you may prove what the will of God is, that which is **good** and **acceptable** and **perfect**."* 1 John 2:15 tells us, *"Do not love the world nor the things in the world If anyone loves the world, **the love of The Father is not in him**."* 2 Corinthians 6:14 says, *"What fellowship does **light** have with **darkness**."* A good measure for listening would be to determine that the music we listen to exalts God and concerns the things of God. In this way, we not only please God, but we encounter God's presence while listening to music. What we listen to with our ears matters.

---

[5] Chilton, M. (2019). *The Devil Has All the Best Tunes: How Musicians Discovered Their Dark Side*. Udiscovermusic. Retrieved November 7, 2019 from https://www.udiscovermusic.com/in-depth-features/the-devil-has-all-the-best-tunes/.

[6] Arkyn, D. (2015). *Music Industry Exposed Part 1 – Misuse and Abuse of Esoteric Symbols*. The Conscious Reporter. Retrieved November 7, 2019 from http://consciousreporter.com/war-on-consciousness/misuse-and-abuse-of-esoteric-symbols/.

[7] Ibid.

Guard the ears.

One thing leads to another. In other words, one breach in purification will cause other breakdowns toward defilement in us. For instance, if we do not guard our minds, our hearts can be tainted. At all times, we must be watchful of what we do, what we look at with our eyes, what we embrace in our hearts, what we welcome into our minds, what we choose to listen to with our ears, and what we say out of our mouths. When this purification process is followed, it leads to holiness.

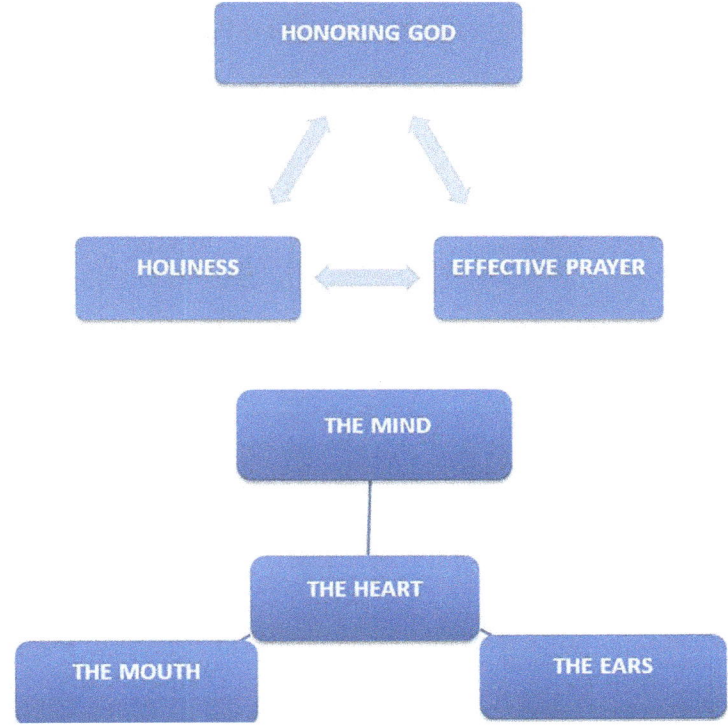

As seen in this illustration, each of our senses affects our course of refinement. Our behaviors and actions are important to living a holy life, establishing effective prayer, and, ultimately, honoring God.

Holiness

This cannot be stressed enough. The enemy Satan is always on a contentious assignment to entice, influence, and misdirect us. So, at all times, we must be watchful of what we do, what we look at with our eyes, what we embrace in our hearts, what we welcome into our minds, what we listen to with our ears, and what we say with our mouths. The enemy knows that when this purification process is applied, it leads to holiness.

1 Thessalonians 5:22 also says, *"Avoid **negativity, impurity,** and all **appearances of evil** in this world.* "Apart from impurity, there is certainly a **better way**—a **deeper way**—in God. You see, God is looking for a **holy vessel**, one consecrated and disciplined enough to acknowledge when guarding needs to take place. He is a holy and righteous God. 1 Peter 1:16 says, *"Be ye **HOLY**, for **I AM HOLY**."* Meditating on Scripture and purifying our hearts daily is critical. Even if we concentrate on the condition of our heart at the beginning of prayer, this can open the door to divine purification and communion with God. James 5:16 further indicates that the effectual, fervent prayer of a righteous man is very effective. In other words, as we keep ourselves pure and untainted, we are honored and favored by the Lord. Adhering to these disciplines not only leads to holiness, but also sets us up for effective prayer. Therefore, we must honor the authority of God over our lives in all our ways.

Honoring God

We honor God by keeping God first—making sure that we consider God in every portion of our lives. That means ensuring we avoid habitual distractions and hindrances. For instance, we should allow God to lead us instead of relying on our own strength and by frequently communicating with God to be certain that we are pursuing His heart. This includes our behaviors and actions. What we speak with our mouths, what we look at with our eyes, what we entertain in our minds, what we receive into our hearts, and what we listen to with our ears matters to God. The Lord wants more than anything for us all to remain undefiled and separated from the vanities of this world.

Honoring God also means to defend everything that concerns Him—pronouncing His glory and absolute authority over mankind. Any efforts to discredit the almighty God should be immediately denounced. If we do not genuinely honor God, He has a way of bringing us to our knees or forcing us into a corner so we may acknowledge Him the way we should. The present and future of our society is dependent upon how we submit our lives to God and how we reverence Him.

1) Are we genuine or sincere about things that concern God?
2) How do we treat others and how do we legitimately view God?
3) Have we honestly sought to please God and not ourselves?

Self-reflection is paramount. Will we adhere to the will of God? And do our lips correlate with what our hearts demonstrate? Matthew 15:8-9 says, *"These people honor Me with their lips, but their hearts are far from Me. They worship me in vain; their teachings are merely human rules."*

Chapter 8

A NEED FOR HEALING IN THE LAND

Before I even begin this discussion, I can imagine the troubles within the year 2020 that already run through your mind as you read. There is much healing needed within our society. The whole world is intense, and many are in a state of shock regarding what has become of civilization. For example, Coronavirus (COVID-19), mass shootings, extreme hatred, defiance, injustice, decline of the economy, loss of jobs, food lines and famine, etc., have recently all been at the highlight of our concerns. It is a time when we need God the most as we recognize life is so uncertain and filled with so much chaos.

> 2 Timothy 3:1-3 says, *"You must understand that in the **last days** there will come times of **much trouble**. People will love themselves and money. They will have pride and tell of all the things they have done. They will speak against god. Children and young people will not obey their parents. People will not be thankful and they will not be holy. They will not love each other. No one can get along with them. They will tell lies about others. They will not be able to keep from doing things they know they should not do. They will be wild and want to beat and hurt those who are good."*

This, of course, was predicted many years ago. But as we can see, it speaks a lot about today's times. It is a timely and revelatory message in relation to the last days - how evil pronounces itself in the earth regardless of what God has desired for mankind. And when that happens, we must consider the consequences.

I would like to share something with you that occurred on December 29, 2019. After almost an hour during prayer, I kept hearing a horn or a trumpet in the spirit. As I tuned in closer, in the spirit, I saw a vision of a massive amount of people from a distance needing deliverance. They looked destitute and in danger. I asked God what it meant. But at that moment, I didn't get a clear enough answer to understand it all. Yet, I just felt many lives were in jeopardy. And not only were they from a distance, but they were heading in my direction. I also felt God's heart in tears... And He stressed that He has continually reached out to many, but was not pleased with the condition of the hearts of mankind. The intensity of God's sorrow lingered for the last fifteen minutes of my prayer. It was a sign for me regarding upcoming danger. A few weeks later COVID began its spread in America.

According to the scriptures, whenever there is extreme sin and defiance in the land judgment came. And as Kings refused the counsel of God, bad things happened. For instance, God's people, the Israelites, were slaves in Egypt for their rebellion approximately 400 years. Nevertheless, God orchestrated a plan to deliver them from captivity. He sent His servant Moses to Pharaoh, the ruler of Egypt. Moses demanded that Pharaoh release God's people from slavery. However, Pharaoh, of course, didn't listen. As a result, the first plague was sent as a curse into the water - turning into blood. But Pharaoh continued to refuse God's instructions. Instead, he chose to remain defiant in his ways and would not listen. So in the end, God sent another plague that ended up spreading to each of the first born sons of Egypt in which Pharaoh's oldest son died. (Exodus 7-12).

> 2 Chronicles 7:13-15 says, *"At times I might **shut up** the heavens so that **no rain** (no blessing) falls, or command grasshoppers to **devour** your **crops** (economy and famine), or **send plagues** (pandemic) among you."*

That is why it is extremely important for us to acknowledge our ways and adhere to the principles God has imparted to us throughout the scriptures. Of course, we will never be perfect. But we must do everything we can to be right with God. The infection of Coronavirus has devastated many lives and extreme chaos has caused enormous tragedy throughout the land. Some affected by COVID were people of God and some were not. One thing noticed with this virus is that many became infected after they did not safeguard themselves. Others safeguarded themselves, but somehow still succumbed to infection. Nevertheless, the scriptures are clear on how we ought to respond to pandemics.

> Isaiah 26:20 says, *"Go, MY people, enter your **rooms** and **shut** the **doors behind you**; **hide yourselves** for a little while until HIS **wrath** has **passed by**."*

But when we are essential workers or are obligated to perhaps enter public facilities to purchase what we need, we are at the feet of God's mercy. And without a doubt, this is a year we will all remember. It is a time where we have seen the frailty of mankind in the center of a traumatic set of circumstances. However, though the world has been shakened, not all is lost. For instance, there are many people who would have never sought after God if there was no COVID. There were thousands of people who even died on their death beds reaching for God. Many who would have never done so, made it to eternal life in that moment of desperation. Their last breath and the cry of their hearts became the salvation of their souls.

In this season, God is searching the hearts of many... And this is a time not to test Him by remaining defiant, but to acknowledge Him.

We have to know how to identify with the times. God speaks through our circumstances. Sometimes He has to shake things up in order to get our attention. When you look back on all your conflicts of life, can you admit there was definitely some underlying force that preserved you when you couldn't have done it all on your own? In fact, even the strongest people have weak moments and are susceptible to hidden and apparent dangers.

And if God lifts His divine intervention from us, we have no hope. But if it was not for that situation in your life, would you have considered God? If you perhaps had everything going your way, would the focus of your heart towards God be as strong as it is today? The fact is we all have a situation... And God takes those situations and causes us to draw near to Him in the midst of them. Even if it's just our time and we succumb to an illness, at least we would know that we did everything we could to draw near to God. But while we still have breath in our bodies we must yield to the Creator. The time is now. That is the way of wisdom. It is a deeper path for us all especially in the center of such extreme circumstances.

Proverbs 9:10 says, *"The fear of the LORD is the beginning of wisdom, and the knowledge of the Holy One is insight."*

Those who have eyes will see and those who have ears will hear what the Spirit of Jesus declares today. As the anger of the Lord is moving through the land in this season, respect this plague, draw near to God, and don't look back. Remain in the unwavering existence of His presence. Anything short of that is dangerous, destructive, and foolish. Let us honor God and make certain our stance of commitment is sure.

Stay In God's Presence

Beyond what we ever imagined, we are in desperate times. There is no doubt that COVID -19 is devastating and painful to watch as many people cling to their lives. Numerous lives are seeking for help during this pandemic – much chaos and uncertainty for many. But I want to call to remembrance 2 Kings Chapter 5 Verses 1–27 where the prophet Elisha instructed Naaman of Syria to take a bath in the Jordan River. Naaman was a leper of disease. And so, eventually he dipped himself in the Jordan River seven times as Elisha instructed. As a result of that, the Bible says Naaman was miraculously healed. This display of power symbolizes the hand of God over one's life. For instance, water often exemplifies the presence of God as mentioned in Ezekiel 47 and also the many passages where Jesus identifies Himself as water all throughout the scriptures Jhn. 4:14, Rev. 22:1, Rev. 22:17, Isa. 44:3, Isa. 58:11, Isa. 41:17-18).

And so Naaman dipped into the water seven times - seven is the number of perfection. Which means Naaman sought God perfectly. So that's what I want to focus in on as I further discuss this critical topic. Whenever we are in desperate moments, the presence of God is our refuge and we must position ourselves perfectly in pursuit of Him. In the midst of every occasion – especially in dark times such as pestilence and plague, God's presence is the place we ought to dwell.

> Psalms 91:1-3 says, *"Whoever **dwells** in the shelter of the Most High will rest in the shadow of the Almighty. I will say of the LORD, "He is my **refuge** and my **fortress**, my God, in whom I trust. Surely he will save you from the fowler's snare and from the deadly pestilence."*

You might be in a desperate moment right now. You may even be sick. But I urge you to dip yourself into God's presence and keep yourself there. Don't just pray and seek God once in a while. But stay perfectly in His presence. Seek Him extensively and diligently in that secret place. At the same time, we must also examine closely within ourselves to determine what is most honorable in the sight of God. In that, God is pleased and will often draw us closer as He provides adequate direction.

2 Chronicles 7:14 says, *"If MY people, who are called by MY name, will **humble** themselves and **pray** and **seek my face** and **turn from their wicked ways,** then I will **hear** from heaven, and I will **forgive** their **sin** and will **heal** their **land."***

Despite the fact that we are in a pandemic, God is a god that forgives and eventually finds a way to stimulate revival among His people. However, right now we must reverence Him and set our hearts on whatever pleases Him. After all this is over, I believe in my spirit that people will pour into the churches, run to the altar, and seek God like never before. Revival is coming and we as the church must be ready for it. Now is the time to be seeking after God to express our commitment. Extreme circumstances call for extreme measures.

Chapter 9

KNEELING & PRAYER

Reaching out in prayer from our heart and letting go of ourselves, even if we have to lay down on our faces or shout our voices to the rooftops, is an indication of our hunger and thirst for God. In such cases, we should not be concerned about how we look or who is around us. Another very clear demonstration of devotion is kneeling before the Lord. Kneeling in prayer is not necessarily an indication of guilt, but it is most notably the highest declaration of worship at the feet of Jesus one can make. At the same time, kneeling is symbolic of honor, allegiance, and submission. It is a sign of compliance with authority and a clear expression of respect. It is a meaningful gesture of sincerity and desperation that often causes God to illustrate His presence and power on the earth. Of course, if we have an ailment or we are physically impaired in some way, we may not be able to kneel. However, those who are capable should consider kneeling as a necessary act of submission.

Jesus, God the Son, knelt down on His knees in prayer under total submission to God the Father in the Garden of Gethsemane before He was crucified (Luke 22:41-42). While we are imperfect with many flaws that we may not even recognize we have, the Bible says Jesus had absolutely no sin in Him (2 Corinthians 5:21). Yet Jesus, God the Son, having no sin, still bowed down on His knees to give honor and reverence to God the Father. Of course, we can pray anywhere at any time, but it is a special moment when we bow down on our knees to pray.

Romans 14:11 says, *"For it is written, 'As I live, says the Lord, every knee shall bow to me, and every tongue shall confess to God.'"* Psalm 95:6 says, *"O come, let us worship and bow down: let us kneel before the LORD our maker."* Daniel kneeled upon his knees three times a day to pray and give thanks before his God (Daniel 6:10). 2 Chronicles 20:18 says, *"Jehoshaphat bowed with his face to the ground, and all the people of Judah and Jerusalem fell down in worship before the LORD."*

1 Kings 8:54 says, *"When Solomon had finished praying this entire prayer and supplication to the LORD, he arose from before the altar of the LORD, from kneeling on his knees with his hands spread toward heaven."* True worship begins with reaching out to God…not always initiating a short prayer, not always praying while we are sitting or standing…but by kneeling down before God and honoring Him. Just imagine if God came down in His fullness…we would not be able to withstand the fullness of His presence. In fact, because we are not yet in our spiritual bodies, our fleshly bodies would run from the power of His presence. Moses had to stand behind a rock and God had to turn His back to Moses in order for Moses to handle even a glimpse of Him. Exodus 33:21-22 says, *"And the LORD said, 'Behold, there is a place by me where you shall stand on the rock, and while my glory passes by I will put you in a cleft of the rock, and I will cover you with my hand until I have passed by."*

Can you imagine the awesome glory of the Lord? Yet, we are made from the dust of the earth, as we see when Genesis 2:7 says, *"Then the LORD God formed a man from the dust of the ground and breathed into his nostrils the breath of life, and the man became a living being."* Therefore, we as mortals made by the Creator must acknowledge the absolute power that stems from Him. One who is true to God will reverence the extremity of His splendor and authority over their lives. These are the reasons why it is significant that we demonstrate deeper levels of admiration and esteem towards God—including in times of prayer. Let us continue to bow down before Him. He is not dishonored, but He is the honorable Almighty! If we were to see God face to face in all His magnificence and array of glory, we would want to bow down at

His feet. We must continue to seek Him diligently from the heart. He promises, *"You will seek me and find me, when you seek me with all your heart"* (Jeremiah 29:11-13). And you shall. Finding the deeper things of God requires some level of determination.

Prayer & God's Presence

There is a fine line between complacency and religion. God doesn't want us to be complacent, and He doesn't want us to just be religious. He desires a deep relationship with us. It is a place in the spirit that is unforgettable; however, getting there takes some effort. One day as I meditated on the Lord, He began to speak to me. He said, "When My people have sought Me with a sincere and diligent heart, My divine presence will be revealed unlike what they have already encountered. Many seek Me on the weekends to reverence Sunday, but they have not sought Me during the week. Their hearts are filled with things that are contrary to Me. They have not honored My way. Still I have sought after them with My counsel. My heart is angered and grieved. Yet I seek them with a full heart of commitment in return."

Seeking God in prayer and being devoted to His way of life for us is vital. In Genesis, the first thing that mankind received in the garden was God's presence. Several decades later, Israel built God's temple, but discontinued their communion with God by not remaining active and consistent enough to find His presence. Ezekiel 10:4 indicates how God's glory left the temple due to the slothfulness of His people. We must be dedicated and persistent in seeking God's presence. In fact, God's spirit is more effective when the full Body of Christ is actively engaged in prayer. Deuteronomy 32:30 mentions that one can chase a thousand and two can put ten thousand to flight. In other words, you may be mighty in prayer alone, but you can be even mightier with others joining you. When the Body of Christ is united in prayer, the move of God is activated.

Prayer is essential...We cannot legitimately participate in any ministry or spiritual journey without it and it is a genuine effort to find God's presence. Prayer emphasizes one's willingness to be closer to God and to establish a meaningful relationship with the creator of life. 1 Thessalonians 5:17 says, *"Pray without ceasing."* God wants us to pray and mean it. To have a closer relationship with God, we must begin to pray deeper and make our prayers touch God. That means not being complacent with religious ritual, but finding God on a different level than just uttering a short prayer or attending a Sunday service. It is sort of like digging for gold—the more you dig, the more you find. Hebrews 11:6 says, *"For without faith it is impossible to please Him; he who cometh to God must know and believe who He is and that He is a rewarder to those who diligently seek Him."* You see, there are different levels of God's presence. God's presence is deeper than the ocean. Ezekiel 47 mentions the presence of God through an illustration of an outpouring of water inside the temple. The fact is that God's presence is an outpouring without limits. If we are complacent, we will miss out on the glory of the Lord. Nevertheless, God does not want us to ever feel forced to pray; He wants us to wholeheartedly desire Him...His heart yearns for it. Many times in prayer, I have discerned that He desires the hunger of prayer among His people.

Prayer results in effective communication between us and God. Prayer should not be a ritual, but a communication from heart to heart—our heart to God's heart. However, prayer does need some sort of structure. The following structure of prayer may be helpful:

1) **Heart Meditation** – The purpose is to ensure that our hearts are pure before we come into God's presence in prayer. For example, if someone has offended us, we are to meditate in our hearts on loving that individual so that we can follow His mandate regarding loving others and come before Him in prayer with a pure heart. Psalm 19:14 says, *"Let the words of my mouth and the meditation of my heart be acceptable in your sight, O Lord, my rock and my redeemer."*

2) **Exalt God with praise.** – This shows God is openly honored and reverenced. Exalting Him with words of admiration, gratitude, or singing invites God into our midst. Psalm 86:12 says, *"I will give thanks to you, O lord my God with my whole heart, and I will glorify your name forever."*

3) **Pray in the Spirit.** – For those who have the Holy Ghost, this is to ensure that we are aligned with God in communication through our heavenly language, speaking in tongues. However, those who do not have the evidence of speaking in tongues can pray unto God fervently from their hearts. 1 Corinthians 14:2 says, *"For he that speaketh in an unknown tongue speaketh not unto men, but unto God: for no man understandeth him; howbeit in the spirit he speaketh mysteries."*

4) **Listen for God's voice.** – Listening ensures we have completed the communication process with God. In fact, it makes sense to listen after we speak. Oftentimes, if we walk away without listening for God's voice, we miss His leading at that particular moment. Proverbs 3:6 (MSG) says, *"Listen for God's voice in everything you do, everywhere you go; he's the one who will keep you on track."*

5) **Open up the Bible.** – Doing so shows God is able to communicate all He wants to say to us. For instance, if God

does not speak to us during or after prayer, He will often speak to us through His holy Word. Psalm 119:105 says, *"Thy word is a lamp unto my feet, and a light unto my path."* The more time we spend with God, the more of His presence He will reveal to us. Without diligence, there is no progress; lacking progress disrupts the movement of God in our lives. Praying and finding God's presence is the essence of life. Let us be diligent in communication with God through prayer. We must value our time with God. Pray without ceasing, lengthen your prayers when possible, and pray fervently with a sincere heart of submission; seeking God ignites His Spirit in our lives.

Chapter 10

THE HOLY SPIRIT

fter the fall of man into sin, God perceived mankind to be in great need of redemption. Therefore, He took a portion of Himself as deliverance, and it manifested itself as Jesus Christ. Jesus Christ then perceived mankind in need of a great sense of empowerment. So He took a portion of Himself as a guide, and it manifested itself as the **Holy Ghost**. It is the **Fire of God** that **burns** from within—it **moves you**.

Matthew 3:11 is where John the Baptist said, *"I indeed **baptize you** in water unto repentance: but He (Jesus) that cometh after me is **mightier** than I, whose shoes I am **not** worthy to bear: He shall **baptize you** in **The Holy Spirit** and in **fire**."* That fire is the **outpouring** and the **anointing** of **the Spirit of God** upon His people. In the New Testament, the Holy Spirit is recognized as one of the most divine revelations discussed in the Bible. This gift is identified as a stimulation of spiritual power and boldness to become witnesses for Jesus Christ" (2 Corinthians 3:12). Christ dwelled in the Body of Christ to direct, lead, teach, and empower His people to reach the lost and to uphold the ideal guidelines

of holiness. Acts 4:31 says, *"After they prayed, the place where they were meeting was shaken. And they were all **filled** with **The Holy Spirit** and spoke the Word of God **boldly**."* We also see in John 14:16, *"And I will pray the Father, and he shall give you another Comforter, that he may abide with you forever"* And verse 26 of the same chapter tells us, *"But the Comforter, which is the Holy Ghost, whom the Father will send in my name, he shall teach you all things, and bring all things to your remembrance, whatever I have said to you."* For that reason alone, it is imperative that Christians are filled with the Baptism of the Holy Spirit; Jesus even declared that it was highly significant for us Christians.

Jesus says in John 3:5, *"I tell you the truth, no one can enter the kingdom of God unless he is born of water and the Spirit. Flesh gives birth to human life, but the Spirit gives birth to spiritual life. You should not be surprised at my saying, 'You must be born again.'"*

Acts 1:8 says, *"But you shall receive power, after that the Holy Ghost is come on you: and you shall be witnesses to me both in Jerusalem, and in all Judaea, and in Samaria, and to the uttermost part of the earth."* Matthew 28:19 says, *"Go you therefore, and teach all nations, baptizing them in the name of the Father, and of the Son, and of the Holy Ghost."* Acts 2:2-4 tells us, *"Suddenly a **sound** like a **mighty rushing wind** came from **heaven** and filled the whole house where they were sitting. They saw what seemed to be tongues of **fire** (Holy fire of God) that separated and came to rest on each of them. All of them were filled with The Holy Ghost and began to speak in other tongues as the Spirit enabled them."*

God wants spiritual growth for His people and for the churches. He wants us to operate out of our spirits and not our flesh. God wants to manifest the gifts of the Spirit through us. Right now, as we speak, He's building up disciples. He wants to birth something out of you as well. He wants to use those who are willing to be used, as no one will receive the baptism of the Holy Ghost and spiritual gifts if there is no desire to use them for God. God responds to our desire to be used, making ourselves available to be used by God and depending completely on Him to stimulate our spiritual gifts by drawing closer to Him. The more we reach in the Spirit, the more God reveals Himself and manifests His glory in the midst of His people.

In the year 2000, when I first started seeking God, I wanted to be baptized by the Holy Ghost. So I made sure I was baptized by water, and the pastor submerged me into the water (Matthew 28:19). Then I pursued the fire baptism of the Holy Ghost (Acts 1:8, 2:4 & 2:38), which came four months later. This was a very sentimental time for me because this was when God began to pour His anointing into my life. To explain my experience, I will tell you about when I attended a church revival. I went up to the altar with several others who were urgently seeking God as well. Without hesitation, I lifted my hands up and reached out to God in deep prayer. Then all of a sudden, I started speaking in another language (speaking in tongues). I felt a sense of empowerment and boldness for the Lord I can't explain. It was life changing. Since that day, I have fluently spoken in tongues when I pray, as my heavenly language unto God. Understand also that when you speak in tongues, the enemy Satan cannot understand you and you are in divine communication and connection with the almighty God.

A deep zeal of fire burns from within me now for the Lord. God imparts boldness within His people to fight vigilantly for His statutes and for His precepts. The Holy Ghost directs us through all things and ignites this deep passion of God within our hearts (Luke 24:32). It stimulates us and impels us to speak of God to others with boldness. The Holy Ghost is an agent of sanctification and produces purity, truth, and godly purpose in our lives. God's intent is to draw us closer as we desire to know Him more.

Titus 2:14 says, *"(Jesus Christ) He who gave Himself for us to **redeem us** from **all wickedness** and to **purify** for Himself a people that are His **very own, eager to do what is good**."* Fire is a great visualization of the work of the Holy Spirit. In Matthew 3:11, John the Baptist says, *"I baptize you with water for repentance, but He who is coming after me is mightier than I, whose sandals I am not worthy to carry. He will baptize you with the **Holy Spirit** and with **fire**."* That manifestation dwells in our hearts (Romans 8:9). Moreover, according to American Bible scholar and Christian theologian Charles C. Ryrie (2019), the Spirit of God is like a fire as He brings God's presence, passion, and purity into the lives of believers.[8] His fire draws us near, cleanses us, refines us, and draws others near to Him as well through His willing vessels. Embrace the fire of God upon your life. God uses people to establish His church and to encourage His people. If you have not yet received the baptism of the Holy Ghost, ask God to fill you with His spirit and be empowered to do the work of the Lord (Acts 1:8 and 2:4).

Those of you who are filled, keep pressing into God with humbleness of heart and boldness that comes with that empowerment. In fact, those of you with pulpit callings will encounter a great sense of urgency to speak for the Lord. For example, you may have a desire to lead a Bible study, to preach or to somehow be more vocal for the church. On the other hand, others may not be called to pulpit ministry even if you are filled with God's Spirit; but there is certainly a purpose for you in the Body of Christ. No matter what, allow God to use you at the capacity He gives you. Philippians 2:13 says, *"For it is God who works in you, both to will and to work for his good pleasure."* 1 Thessalonians 5:24 says, *"Faithful is He who calls you, and He also will bring it to pass."* Hebrews 13:21 says, *"May he equip you with all you need for doing his will. May he produce in you, through the power of Jesus Christ, every good thing that is pleasing to him. All glory to him forever and ever! Amen."*

Purposes of the Holy Spirit

The Holy Spirit is strategic in bringing you and others closer to Christ. It is a journey filled with God's great sense of empowerment comprised of His holy presence. With the many challenges Christians face, the Holy Spirit is essential in combatting countless evil influences and

---

[8] Phillips, S. (2018). *The Mystery Hidden in Shachah: The Hebrew Word for Worship.* Living Word Discovery. Retrieved November 5, 2019 from http://livingwordin3d.com/discovery/2018/02/25/the-mystery-hidden-in-shachah-the-hebrew-word-for-worship/.

defiant behaviors. Titus 2:12 says, *"Training us to renounce ungodliness and worldly passions, and to live self-controlled, upright, and godly lives in the present age."* Matthew 28:19 also says, *"Therefore go and make disciples of all nations, baptizing them in the name of The Father and of The Son and of The Holy Spirit, and teaching them to obey everything I have commanded you. And surely I am with you always, to the very end of the age."*

Various functions of the Holy Spirit are used to manifest divine direction and enablement for God's people. The Holy Spirit orchestrates strategies for helping us reach the fulfillment of our assignments on the earth. Those manifestations are as follows:

1) The Spirit convicts the world of sin, righteousness, and judgment (John 16:8).
2) The Spirit guides us into all truth (John 16:13).
3) The Spirit glorifies and testifies of Christ (John 15:26; 16:14).
4) The Spirit leads us (Romans 8:14; Galatians 5:18; Matthew 4:1; Luke 4:1).
5) The Spirit sanctifies us (2 Thessalonians 2:13; 1 Peter 1:2; Romans 5:16).
6) The Spirit empowers us (Luke 4:14; 24:49; Romans 15:19; Acts 1:8).
7) The Spirit fills us (Ephesians 5:18; Acts 2:4; 4:8, 31; 9:17).
8) The Spirit teaches us to pray (Romans 8:26-27; Jude 1:20).
9) The Spirit bears witness in us that we are children of God (Romans 8:16).
10) The Spirit produces in us the fruit or evidence of His work and presence (Galatians 5:22-23).
11) The Spirit distributes spiritual gifts and manifestations (the outshining) of His presence to and through the body (1 Corinthians 12:4, 8-10; Heb. 2:4).
12) The Spirit anoints us for ministry (Luke 4:18; Acts 10:38).
13) The Spirit sets us free from the law of sin and death (Romans 8:2).

14) The Spirit reveals the deep things of God to us (1 Corinthians 2:10).

15) The Spirit reveals what has been given to us from God (1 Corinthians 2:12).

16) The Spirit dwells in us (Romans 8:9; 1 Corinthians 3:16; 2 Timothy 1:14; John 14:17).

17) The Spirit speaks to, in, and through us (1 Corinthians 12:3; 1 Timothy 4:1; Revelation 2:11; Hebrews 3:7; Matthew 10:20; Acts 2:4; 8:29; 10:19; 11:12, 28; 13:2; 16:6,7; 21:4,11).

18) The Spirit transforms us into the image of Christ (2 Corinthians 3:18).

19) The Spirit gives us access to God the Father (Ephesians 2:18).

20) The Spirit confesses that Jesus came in the flesh (1 John 4:2).

21) The Spirit teaches us (1 Corinthians 2:13; John 14:26).

22) The Spirit gives us joy (1 Thessalonians 1:6).

23) The Spirit enables some to preach the gospel (1 Peter 1:12).

24) The Spirit moves us (2 Peter 1:21).

25) The Spirit casts out demons (Matthew 12:28).

26) The Spirit brings things to our remembrance (John 14:26).

27) The Spirit comforts us (Acts 9:31).

28) The Spirit brings unity and oneness to the church (Ephesians 4:3; 2:14-18).

Here, the Holy Spirit plays the same role that He plays in the Godhead. The Spirit is the life that unites Father and Son. The Spirit plays the same role in the church; when the Holy Spirit is operating in a group of people, He unites them in love. Therefore, a sure evidence of the Holy Spirit working in a group is love and unity. Signs and wonders are not clear signs of the Holy Spirit, unless we operate in love.

In conclusion, the Holy Spirit unites us to Jesus Christ and to His church. He is essential to our walk with the Lord. The Spirit reveals Christ to us, gives us His life, and makes Christ alive in us. The Spirit reveals the experiences of Jesus and shows us how to emulate His qualities. It is a purification process in which God pours His knowledge and wisdom into us in order to bring us through our expected journey. So, overall, the Holy Spirit empowers us to do the work of the Lord to give Him pleasure and absolute **glory** in the earth. The glory of the Holy Spirit stems from something much higher than what we are imparted as Christians. Only God Himself is the source of godly empowerment.

There Is No Inner God—Jesus Is Lord

We must not be side-tracked with spiritual development contrary to the scriptures. A rebellious spirit is sweeping across the nation and throughout the world concerning an inner god. It's a perspective or notion of a person being able to tap into some sort of internal energy, while ignoring the almighty God of the Scriptures. But the Word of God declares in John 1:1-3, *"In the beginning was the Word, and the Word was with God, and the Word **was God**. He was with God in the beginning. **Through him all things were made; without him nothing was made that has been made."** John 1:10-12 further says, **"He was in the world, and though the world was made through Him, the world did not recognize Him. He came to His own, and His own people did not receive Him."** And Jesus said in John 14:6, "I Am The Way and The Truth and The Life. No man comes unto the father except through Me."*

Jesus is the authority of all. And whoever denounces His righteousness shall also be denounced on the Day of Judgment. Mankind has many flaws, so how would anyone (besides Jesus being immortal) be able to justify being a god if mankind is a mortal being? The question is, did mankind create itself? Is man able to prevent his own death? Can he deliver himself from captivity or bondage? How about raising himself from the dead? God's Word warns us to be aware of anyone who rejects the Gospel of Jesus. 2 Timothy 3:5 warns, *"Having a form of godliness but denying its power. Have nothing to do with such people."*

This type of spirit is unruly and defiant—a spirit that rejects Jesus, seeks power only from within, says whatever it wants to say, and does whatever it wants to do. At the same time, this spirit disregards consideration toward others, hates what is good, and embraces what is evil. Moreover, it is a spirit that overlooks immoral behavior, gives no room for instruction, and does not desire to yield to any rules. 1 John 4:3 says, *"But every spirit that does not acknowledge Jesus is not from God. This is the spirit of the Antichrist, which you have heard is coming and even now is already in the world."*

Pray to defeat this spirit, as it dishonors the very existence of God. If people would only abide by the Lord's precepts and adhere to His ways, they would perhaps share profound and impactful experiences that others often mention. If they would humble themselves and pray and turn from their wicked ways, they would hear from heaven that Jesus is Lord (2 Chronicles 7:14). Everyone has an opportunity to encounter the only true God and to see His absolute glory and power within their reach. However, there are many who have turned away from the faith and sought after their own selfish desires and lifestyles. As a result, it is most unfortunate that they have wondered away from the truth. Acknowledging God is a matter of keeping the flesh under subjection—adhering to the righteous path He has laid out for us.

Jesus Was God in the Flesh

The fact is that our flesh is not as tolerant as the Spirit of God when contending with the cares of this world. The Scriptures mention the spirit is willing, but the flesh is weak (Matthew 26:40-43). Jesus Himself had a well-rounded understanding of how difficult it is for one to suffer in the flesh. As God and man, He not only suffered but also had the power to release Himself from it—but chose not to.

> *For to us a child is born, to us a son is given, and the government will be **on His shoulders**. And he will be*

*called Wonderful Counselor, **Mighty God**, Everlasting Father, Prince of Peace.* (Isaiah 9:6)

*Behold! The virgin will conceive a child! She will give birth to a son, and they will call him Immanuel, which means **"God is with us."*** (Matthew 1:23)

In the beginning was the Word, and the Word was with God, and the Word WAS GOD (Jesus). He was with God in the beginning. Through him all things were made; without him nothing was made that has been made. (John 1:1-3)

*He **was in the world**, and though the world was **made through Him**, the world did not recognize him. He came to his own, and **His own people did not receive Him.** Yet to all who did receive him, to those who believed in his name, he gave the right to become children of God.* (John 1:10-12)

I and My Father are One. (John 10:30)

*Jesus answered, "I AM the way and the truth and the life. No one comes to the Father **except through Me.** If you really know me, you will know my Father as well. From now on, you do know him and have seen him."* (John 14:6-7)

*Jesus answered: "Don't you know me, Philip, even after I have been among you such a long time? **Anyone who has*** *seen Me has seen The Father. how can you say, show us The Father?"* (John 14:9-10)

*Even the **Spirit Of Truth**; whom the world cannot receive, because it seeth him not, neither knoweth him: but ye know him; for he **dwelleth with you**, and **shall be in you**. I will not leave you comfortless: I will come to you.** (John 14:17-18)

*Thomas said to him, **"My Lord, my God!"** Then Jesus told him, "Because you have seen me, you have believed; blessed are those who have not seen and yet have believed."* (John 20:28-29)

*Yet for us there is **one God, The Father, from whom are all things and for whom we exist, and one Lord Jesus Christ, from whom are all things and for whom we exist**.* (1 Corinthians 8:6)

That at the name of Jesus every knee should bow, in heaven and on earth and under the earth, and every tongue acknowledge that Jesus Christ is Lord, to the glory of God the Father. (Philippians 2:10)

*While we wait for the blessed hope—the appearing of **the glory of our great God and Savior, Jesus Christ.*** (Titus 2:13)

*Simon Peter, a servant and apostle of Jesus Christ, To those who through the righteousness of **our God and Savior Jesus Christ** have received a faith as precious as ours.* (2 Peter 1:1)

In retrospect, God in all His power extracted a portion of Himself and Jesus was manifested. Jesus took out a portion of Himself and the Holy Ghost was manifested. As a result, the revelation of God the Father, God the Son, and God the Holy Ghost was revealed. In other words, they are identified as one God, operating in three different functions. For example, water, ice, and vapor are manifested differently but are all one. 1 John 5:7 says, *"For there are three that bear record in heaven, **The FATHER**, **The Word (JESUS)**, and **The HOLY GHOST**: and these **three** are **One**."* They are all one, serving three different functions in order to reach and establish intimacy with mankind. Jesus was not a spirit; He was a man in the flesh—but also God, who died for mankind as a man and was raised again.

Some people today, just as the Pharisees did long ago, deny the Trinity and the deity of Christ. The Pharisees denied the physical resurrection of Christ and salvation by grace alone. But the Scriptures tell us to acknowledge the Godhead of Jesus. 1 John 4:3 says, *"But every spirit that does not acknowledge Jesus has not come in the flesh. This is the spirit of the anti-Christ, which you have heard is coming and even now is already in the world."* Essentially, God chose to come down to our extremely limited environment, although He did not need to. Yet, He humbled Himself unto death and demonstrated His love for all mankind. Ultimately, He rose from the grave and is alive today because He is God. He is our God the creator, God in the flesh, and God in Spirit. His very nature proves He is the almighty God and that He is not limited to the standards of man. He has no source, and He is who He is—despite the finite minds of mortal men. Unlike mankind, God has no restrictions on how He operates or chooses to manifest Himself to others. Jesus is God.

Chapter 11

THE SPIRIT OF JEZEBEL

Unfortunately, various disturbances and conflicts also exist in the earth. Wicked influences are derived from evil forces that are systematically aimed at interfering with the move of God between people. One of those underlying spirits is a principality spirit known as Jezebel. The Bible talks about spiritual forces of evil in the heavenly realms, and Jezebel is one of those, along with Leviathan, Python, and others.

In the book of Kings, Jezebel was a queen who had priests killed because of their refusal to follow her pagan religion (1 Kings 18:4, NIV). Ephesians 6:12 says, *"For our struggle is not against flesh and blood, but against the rulers, against the authorities, against the powers of this dark world and against the spiritual forces of evil in the heavenly realms."* Donald Ibbitson from Above and Beyond Christian Counseling specifies that Jezebel directs earthly (first heaven) demons to bring damage and destruction to God's people. According to Ibbitson, both men and women can be manipulated by this evil spirit

(2018).[9] It has been responsible for tearing down churches, pastors, prophetic ministries, and other Christian ministries. Similarly, Bible Scholar, Michael Bradley (2018) points out that the spirit of Jezebel has been responsible for breaking up many marriages, friendships, and companies, along with getting many people to commit cold-blooded murders and suicides. [10] Bradley further indicates that this spirit is cunning, intelligent, vicious, and more evil than some of the other lower-ranking demons. Revelations 2:19-20 says, *"I know your deeds, your love and faith, your service and perseverance, and that you are now doing more than you did at first. Nevertheless, I have this against you: You tolerate that woman Jezebel, who calls herself a prophet. By her teaching, she misleads my servants into sexual immorality and the eating of food sacrificed to idols."* Jezebel targets the headship of ministries. A person with a Jezebel spirit will lie and sows seeds of discord by turning people against each other privately, and individually, behind closed doors. They play the victim, criticizing everyone, especially when they can't manipulate their victims. Mostly, the Jezebel spirit is threatened by prophetic people, simply because they can often be pinpointed when spiritual disruption occurs.

This spirit especially hates men and women of God who are faithfully doing the work of God. It will come in the church to pollute it and quench the flow of the Holy Spirit. If it invades a weak church, there will begin to be little revelation of God's Word during sermons and barely any testimonies. The church will lack the undeniable power of the Holy Spirit and exhibit a decline in spiritual growth; such a church would need to be strong in prayer to recover. A Jezebel spirit usually comes through those who will knowingly or unknowingly involve themselves in forms of witchcraft, in order to make sure they quench the Holy

---

[9]   Ibbitson, D. (2018). *12 Warning Signs That a Person Is Under the Influence of a Jezebel Spirit.* Above & Beyond Christian Counseling. Retrieved September, 5, 2019 from https://aandbcounseling.com/12-warning-signs-person-influence-jezebel-spirit/.

[10]   Bradley, M. (2018). *What Is Jezebel Spirit and How It Operates.* Bible Knowledge. Retrieved September 4, 2019 from https://www.bible-knowledge.com/the-jezebel-spirit-and-how-it-operates/.

Spirit. They typically operate through jealousy, pride, envy, or hatred. They hate humility and love to be adored by others—never seeking to lower themselves. According to theologians, such people are capable of killing others or destroying lives (Bradley, 2018). Nevertheless, we are given all power and authority over evil (Luke 10:19). So not only are we responsible for being watchful of these snares, but we must also defend against them through prayer. 2 Corinthians 2:11 says, *"In order for us to not be outsmarted by Satan, we must be aware of his schemes."*

I have seen this spirit operate through people, including within some churches. It causes divisions among brethren, disrupts unity, stirs up gossip, harbors envy, and clouds the vision of others with much confusion. That is why no matter what, we must forgive and genuinely support one another without yielding to such levels of controversy. Nonetheless, the enemy will be subdued by the **hand of God,** as we move with the Lord's leading and authority in the earth. Isaiah 59:19 tells us, *"So shall they fear the name of the Lord from the west, and His Glory from the rising of the sun. When the enemy shall come in like a flood,* **The Spirit Of The LORD** *shall* **lift up** *a* **standard against** *him."* Know what you are up against in this world. Whether we serve God or not, this is the reality. We must make sure Jesus resides in our corner and stands with us in the midst of the forces that surround us.

Spiritual Warfare

Good against evil in the spiritual realm is real. Spiritual warfare is not something we choose to encounter, but it's something that exists more often than most people realize. All throughout the Bible, there is a strong indication of good and evil. For instance, we can perceive darkness contending against the light whenever God presented His plan for mankind and it was eventually disobeyed. It is a constant battle that began in the days of Adam and Eve (Genesis 3:1-24, EST), continued all the way to when Jesus was rejected in Matthew 26:47-56 (NIV), and will continue until the end of the scriptures that describe the Battle of Armageddon during the second coming of Christ (Revelation 15 &16, NIV).

Another example is when Satan asked God for permission to attack Job (Job 1:9-11, NIV), we can see that evil was clearly working against Job, based on the opposing situations mounted up around him. However, as a result of Job's submission to God in the face of his circumstances, God delivered him from his troubles. In addition, when King David fell spiritually as a result of giving in to physical temptation when he looked upon Bathsheba (who was already married) and pursued her, we know there must have been some hidden force behind David sinning against God. It happened because of some sort of evil influence (2 Samuel 11:2-27, NSRV).

The fact is that even Jesus Himself met spiritual warfare when He was tempted by Satan as He fasted in the wilderness (Matthew 4:1-11, NLT). Jesus also faced the enemies' opposition when He carried out His ministry and performed miracles, signs and wonders upon the earth. Yet it didn't start there with Satan contending with Jesus. When the word of the Lord was fulfilled that Jesus would be born as a Messiah into Bethlehem (Matthew 2:6, NLT), we know that there was some evil force at work behind the scenes to hinder that experience. And as we know, anything God favors, Satan hates. So we then see King Herod sending soldiers to kill any baby boy who could have been the baby Jesus in Bethlehem, as Jesus escapes into Egypt with Mary and Joseph (Matthew 2:13-14, EST).

During Jesus' ministry, He and His disciples experienced extreme opposition. We can clearly see how the enemy sought to hinder His efforts. We also see the effects of evil and how people were influenced to do evil, even when good openly presented itself to them. Regardless of the love for humanity Jesus demonstrated to everyone, the people still chose to crucify Jesus instead of the murderer Barabbas (John 18:40, ESV). Therefore, we as people of God must understand that because we are followers of our risen Lord Jesus, that evil will often contend with us in many forms. In fact, we don't get to choose whether we are involved in spiritual warfare; it is something that is already in motion against us. These types of manifestations concerning good or evil are revealed through people or circumstances today. Spiritual defiance and opposing forces are still obvious.

Even more importantly, as intercessors, we must realize that our prayers are extremely vital. Through prayer, we establish a deep relationship with God. Through prayer, God draws near to His people. Through prayer, we move God to intervene for a cause or circumstance. Through prayer, we can communicate many personal needs within our families. Through prayer, we can express several needs for the church. Through prayer, we seek God's divine direction. Through prayer, we oppose all evil and systematically disrupt the enemies' plans—causing them to lose hold those they hold in bondage. The apostle Paul says, *"Pray without ceasing"* (1 Thessalonians 5:17, EST), so Paul knew the significance of continual prayer not only for a deep relationship with God; Paul also knew that prayer stops the enemy from hindering those doing the Lord's work.

Prayer is a form of spiritual warfare—good against evil. So as we pray, let us not focus only on our personal needs, the needs of others, the needs of the church, and the redemption of the world. Most of all, let's pray concerning our rebuke toward the enemy—preventing the enemy from advancing against God's people. Pray for spiritual leaders, pray for the unity between God's people, pray for the overall safety of our nation and various nations around us. Intercessors are required to intercede on behalf of others. However, part of that mission is to pray against attacks from the enemy. Luke 10:19 says, *"Behold, I give unto you power to tread on serpents and scorpions, and over all the power of the enemy: and nothing shall by any means hurt you."*

Intercessory Prayer

The move of God begins with prayer. Whether we pray at home in our prayer rooms, in the church, or on a mountain top, intercessory prayer is a place where we seek the deep presence of God. It is a place where we pursue healing and restoration. It is a place where we encourage and lift up one another. But it can also be a place of training and preparation, where ministers are being raised up as laborers at the front lines of the church, just like the prophet Samuel, who mentored the prophets in the School of the Prophets (1 Samuel 19:19-24). God uses intercessory prayer as a way to teach us how to combat and defend against the enemy.

At the same time, learning through prayer how to reach high in the Spirit to encounter God's divine glory is equally essential. We rise up in faith as we pray so that God will begin to manifest the spiritual gifts within us. We learn how to pray for one another as a unified people. We learn how to trust God in our adversities of life, despite what we see— walking by faith and not by sight. Mark 11:24 says, *"Therefore I say unto you, What things soever ye desire, when ye pray, believe that ye receive [them], and ye shall have [them]."* Psalm 4:3 (NLT) tells us, *"Know that the Lord has set apart his faithful servant for himself; the Lord hears when I call to him."*

Corporate Prayer

We must be sensitive to the spirit enough to know what to pray for and when. But there are various things to pray concerning the move of God in any given situation. Meet your brothers and sisters in Christ at the *frontlines* of battle in *prayer.* Unite in the Spirit and hold up one another in prayer—calling on the Name of the Lord for deliverance and healing in the land.

1 Pray for a *close connection* with God.
2 Pray for your own individual needs—*adversity, hindrances, guidance issues, lack,* etc.
3 Pray for *church organizations* and *effective leadership*.
4 Pray for God's *provision* and *protection* over *all churches*.
5 Pray for *revival, restoration,* and *spiritual renewal* within God's people.

6 Pray for *genuine unity among members*.

7 Pray for the *divine manifestation of God's presence* and the *outpouring of His Spirit*.

8 Pray for *souls to be saved*, *nurtured,* and *discipled.*

9 Pray with *courage against the enemy* and *set a standard against all appearances of evil.*

10 Pray that *more leaders will arise for the Body of Christ.*

11 Pray for this *nation and the other nations around it—justice, repentance, and true direction.*

12 Pray for a *leading from God concerning your true purpose.*

Prayer is extremely essential. When we pray, we move the heart of God causing Him to hearken to our circumstances. If you want some changes in your life, you have to dig **deeper**. If you want to see God move, then you make the **first** move. 1 Chronicles 16:11 says, *"Seek the LORD and His strength, seek His face continually."* Most importantly, let us draw near to God in prayer. Pray for that deep connection. Let us all meet at the throne room of God and look to Him for answers on how to get through the many adversities of life. After all, this is a war in the spiritual realm that quite often manifests itself in the natural.

Spiritual Tenacity

The natural and spiritual realms do not waist time in showing us we need God. The circumstances around us illustrates that without God and His mercy, we are nothing. But understandably, we typically pursue pleasurable moments and desire the things that please us. Without a doubt, God wants us to be joyful and longs to provide the best for His people. However, there are times when we are face to face with adversity. Nevertheless, God strengthens us through the Holy Spirit to overcome. Adversity comes in many forms: disappointment, mistreatment, sickness, and all other types of hardships that are very real in this life. Still, we as people of God are also called to stand firmly during sufferings placed upon us in our daily lives, knowing our lives consist of fighting spiritual battles, no matter how much we would like to deny it. The fact is no one desires to encounter tribulations, and we often long for the easy way of life. However, as mentioned earlier, Jesus demonstrated the victory behind various sufferings. In the same way, patience, longsuffering, perseverance, and faith will create great qualities in anyone diligent enough to overcome. Following Jesus, the apostle Paul also discovered the mystery of suffering. The sufferings of Paul were the following:

1) Bitten by a viper snake (Acts 28:3)
2) Whipped and imprisoned (2 Corinthians 11:23)
3) Beaten, stoned, shipwrecked, a night and a day exposed and floating in the sea (2 Corinthians 11:25)
4) Oppression, painfulness, hunger, thirst, fasting often, cold and nakedness (2 Corinthians 11:27)

Yet Paul said, *"If he will glory, he will glory of the things which concern his infirmities and struggles of life"* (2 Corinthians 11:30). In Romans 8:35-39, he also goes on to say:

> *Who shall separate us from the love of Christ? Shall trouble or hardship or persecution or famine or nakedness or danger or sword? As it is written: "For your sake we face death all day long; we are considered as sheep to be slaughtered." No, in all these things we are more than conquerors through him who loved us.*

Paul also says,

> *For I am convinced that neither death nor life, neither angels nor demons, neither the present nor the future, nor any powers, neither height nor depth, nor anything else in all creation, will be able to separate us from the love of God that is in Christ Jesus our Lord.*

God said to Paul in 2 Corinthians 12:9-10,

> *My grace is sufficient for you, for my power is made perfect in weakness. Therefore Paul said he will boast all the more gladly about his weaknesses, so that Christ's power may rest on him. He said that is why, for Christ's sake, he delights in weaknesses, in insults, in hardships, in persecutions, in difficulties. For when he is weak, then he is strong.*

Paul also said, *"For me to live is Christ, to die is gain"* (Philippians 1:21). Therefore, however a believer dies, in suffering or in relative peace, it is but a transition to "face to face" with the Lord. People of God, James 1:2 says, *"Count it all joy, my brothers, when you meet trials of various kinds."* And Romans 12:12 commands, *"Rejoice in hope, be patient in tribulation, be constant in prayer."* We must realize there is greatness in suffering. In fact, when we have set up our love for God's cause in our sufferings, He will reward us accordingly. If it requires some suffering to encounter the deep manifestation of God's presence, then that's what it takes.

In the year 2002, I lost everything I had. It was a very difficult time in my life, of course. I lost my car and my house; I was unable to see my children very often. I lost my friends, and I was disrespected by those I loved. However, in that, I encountered a very deep and rich relationship with God. It was as if God placed me in a corner and we were face to face—a very divine experience. Following many years of wilderness and tribulation, God restored me in all areas of my life. You see, after He called me into ministry, He then began to test, cleanse, and purge me—chipping away at the rough edges. In my ordeal, I learned to trust in God and embrace the path that He had already determined for me. Hebrews 11:6 says, *"Without faith it is impossible to please Him, and he who comes to God must know and believe who He is, and He is a rewarder to those who diligently seek him."*

The apostle Paul was a man of God who persevered during suffering when perhaps most would not have endured. His reward was deep revelation; anointing that stemmed even from his personal handkerchief; and the power to heal the sick, cast out demons, raise a person from the dead, and impart spiritual gifts by the laying on of hands (Acts 19:11-12). In the midst of our tribulations of misfortune, unusual mistreatment, slander, ridicule, sickness, and all aspects of adversity, we must be still and know who our God is. It is fundamental that we realize God has a purpose in all things concerning His people. The tenacity of our faith is worth more than gold—and is in fact even priceless—as we engage in our encounters against adversity and the harsh reality of spiritual warfare.

> *These trials will show that your faith is genuine. It is being tested as fire tests and purifies gold--though your faith is far more precious than mere gold. So when your faith remains strong through many trials, it will bring you much praise and glory and honor on the day when Jesus Christ is revealed to the whole world.* (I Peter 1:7, NLT)

For that reason, we must endure hardship as good soldiers of Jesus Christ—praying and contending against anything that seeks to dishonor the throne of God. Let us continue to recognize the significance of tenacity in our relationship with God and do whatever it takes to stand firm at the forefront of our warfare. We must remember the men of God before us who suffered much more than we suffer today and determine to be tenacious as we honor God through our persistence. Each time we pray, we enter into a battle of good against evil. When we proclaim the Gospel of Jesus Christ, we enter into adversity with the enemy. Nevertheless, God is faithful and has provided strength through our moments of prayer and tenacity, as we engage in continuous periods of spiritual warfare. Endure! *"You therefore must endure hardship as a good soldier of Jesus Christ"* (2 Timothy 2:3, EST).

Chapter 12

ENCOURAGE ONE ANOTHER

Brothers and sisters in Christ, we must preserve one another with much encouragement. Moreover, it is extremely essential for us to provide others unwavering support without any form of discord or malicious intent. Peacemakers preserve peace and include those around them. We must keep in mind that evil forces in the spiritual realm are actively contending against us to keep us all from running our heavenly courses of salvation. That is why forgiveness in our hearts and maintaining healthy relationships between people will take us a long way. As we guard the mind and the heart from divisional attacks by the enemy, we will not only become unified, but also prevent threats that often disrupt the Body of Christ.

Always employing prayer and supplication for our brothers and sisters is the best practice for adhering to unity. Ultimately, we need to make sure we genuinely support one another spiritually, socially, and emotionally; we must wholeheartedly give one another encouragement at all times, instead of imparting discouragement and unnecessary conflict. We know the enemy is fiercely approaching due to our stance with Christ. However, Jesus said He will build His church and the gates of hell will not prevail against it (Matthew 16:18). Therefore, we must continue to preserve our strength in unity, love, and purity of heart.

Leaders, Encourage Your Members

Where there is a functional community, there is also a good leader. The way in which we lead is just as significant as the leading itself. It takes some skill to guide others in a particular direction. However, leading is not just the measure of clever influence. Ultimately, church leadership involves serving, encouraging, and inspiring others to mature and grow. Essential elements of leadership include determining ways to build up those around you and not forcing them to rely only on you. True leadership is empowering members to develop into established men and women of God. Proverbs 11:14 says, *"For lack of guidance a nation falls, but victory is won through many advisers."* The most significant quality of those serving in authority is character. Without the right character, authority is usually tainted and distorted. If we have a position of authority, we must have clear intentions to serve rather than to be served. Matthew 20:26 declares that whoever wants to become great (leadership responsibility) among God's people must also be a servant. *"Humility is not thinking less of yourself, it's thinking of yourself less."*[11]

We too often see leaders who can cause stagnation in the growth of those who look up to them, if they are not careful. But the fact is that God has given each member a purpose within the Body of Christ, and it is up to leaders to be able to manage these possibilities, as they are accessible. We cannot allow God's movement through His people to be delayed due to neglect and lack of mentorship. In fact, if we as leaders do not know how to mentor our members, let God Himself, through the Holy Spirit, **help others flow into their gifts at the capacity He has given them.** The bottom line is that God desires many to build the church together—not just one or two or even five people. In addition to that, not everyone ministers or provides support for monetary gain—they just want to fulfill their callings. It is a collective

---

[11] Warren, Rick (2002). *"Humility Is Not Thinking Less of Yourself, It's Thinking of Yourself Less."* Brainy Quote. Retrieved August 10, 2019 from https://www.brainyquote.com/quotes/rick_warren_395865.

effort to strengthen members, and God uses various spiritual gifts to accomplish those efforts. 1 Corinthians 12:14 says, *"For the body does not consist of one member, but of many."*

Restrictions within some churches have often caused members to search for other opportunities in order to establish their callings. Some stumble and are faced with the flaws within religious leadership instituted on excessive protocol and limitations. However, when God moves, He does not always move through renowned people. He operates even through the least expected vessel. God seeks to raise up the next David in the midst of warriors. As the Bible mentions in 1 Samuel 17:28-30, David was held back from fighting against the giant Goliath—until he insisted God sent him to fight. The soldiers told David he was not a proper soldier. Nevertheless, God used him to defeat the giant Goliath, and he helped achieve victory for God's people. This is what God will do if we as leaders encourage those around us. Just imagine if you have a number of various warriors cohesively working together to bring God glory. Without a doubt, this is certainly at the core of God's heart.

Leaders to Leaders

There is a great need to emphasize unity among members and leaders, but leaders encouraging other leaders is equally essential. The big picture is that we as leaders are all fighting for the same cause—it's about Jesus. So we must consider the methods of support we use. Do we or do we not give other leaders room to flow in their gifts? We are urged through Scripture to uphold God's people and to work alongside other leaders to establish God's house. Philippians 2:3 says, *"Do nothing out of selfish ambition or vain conceit. Rather, in humility value others above yourselves."* Neglect, mistreatment, competition, envy, and all forms of hindrance have no place in the Body of Christ. We are all created to glorify God in whatever manner He desires. Remember, others encounter the same driving force from God that burns within you. Strategically, see the strength in unity. We cannot fight battles alone and be triumphant.

God sends other leaders to enhance our efforts and to balance ministry functions as needed. When we see other leaders used by God, we should celebrate. Whether they are a part of our church or not, we still need to rejoice over them.

One of the most difficult moments for a man or woman of God is when their own brothers and sisters in Christ don't support them. They are hated by the world for their stance for Christ. They may even be going through difficult circumstances at home. The enemy Satan may be fighting them on every side. Then they come to a fellow Christian for refuge and acceptance into their God-given callings—only to end up empty-handed and neglected. If we are all on the same team, we should be neither neglecting nor competing against our own soldiers. Instead, we should lift up the next person and see God do exploits through them in the power of the Holy Spirit. We are all in this spiritual fight together.

Systemic Hindrance

Throughout many years of walking with the Lord, I have seen these problems in churches. Common barriers exist within our religious institutions. Not only have I personally experienced these issues, but other ministers and preachers have also suffered because of strict rules and guidelines that are laid out for various churches. Men and women who are called, anointed, and gifted have gone through such difficulties. For example, some who have been through many encounters with the Lord and undergone ministerial training programs are still restricted from some religious organizations to exhort or minister. This, of course, is a hindrance for the Body of Christ because sometimes God sends people to assist in facilitating churches with a lack of laborers.

Oftentimes, potential laborers are held back by institutions that set up specific boundaries and guidelines instead of just being led by God. Oftentimes, too much emphasis is focused on the pastor instead of the entire body of members who all have callings on their lives in some way. Our pastors certainly should be reverenced, but we must not forget that they do not always have all the answers. Respecting authority is essential, but an overseer must understand that God has called and chosen many to help establish and raise up His church. Many members within the congregation can contribute to pulpit ministry, as long as God has called them to do so. After all, who put the church together for us all? It was God. It was God who called us and began pouring into us what He desires for us to pour out. It was God who first spoke into our lives and caused us to operate in the Spirit when we didn't even understand it all.

I remember when God first called me into pulpit ministry. I didn't know how to operate, but God kept secretly encouraging me to preach. Then during a Sunday morning service, the church body was in the process of praising God during the worship segment of the service. As I stood listening to the music, the pastor suddenly walked up to me and told me I would be the one to preach the Sunday morning message. Naturally, I was terrified because I felt inadequate and unqualified. But in my spirit, I knew I had to believe in God. So I began to pray internally and sought to desperately find a word from God through the Scriptures. I knew I had only about seven minutes before I would have to deliver God's Word to the congregation. When the time came, I stood up and walked to the podium. Terrified, I grabbed the microphone—but something began to happen inside of me. And when I opened my mouth, it was like a fire burned within my spirit. The message I spoke was not from me, nor was it due to an extensive ministerial education; it came through the power of God that moved through me to deliver a word for His people.

Now, I will be the first one to tell you that the study of God's Word is paramount, and we need to have the knowledge of God flowing within. But I will also be the first to tell you that God can speak through whomever He chooses. It does not matter if a person has acquired a high school diploma or a doctoral degree or a ministerial certificate. What matters is that God fills a man with His Spirit, calls that man, and empowers him for service. Leaders, I urge you to be careful about turning away those who have God's anointing flowing through them simply because the rules of a church organization limits their access. Make sure you have not exalted yourself above what God is trying to do in the midst of your ministry. It's not all about one, two, or three people. It's about God's army He is raising up right in front of you.

During prayer, I asked God for a word concerning this topic, so He swiftly and precisely took me to the following passage:

> *"Get yourself ready!* **Stand up** *and* **say to them whatever I command you**. *Do not be terrified by them, or I will terrify you before them. Today I have made you a fortified city, an iron pillar and a bronze wall to stand against the whole land—against the Kings of Judah, its* **officials**, *its* **Priests** *and* **the people** *of the land. They will fight against you but will not overcome you, for I am with you and will rescue you," declares the Lord.* (Jeremiah 1:17-19)

So this message has been prayed over. It is certainly a real issue and a shattering discomfort for those called by God and, at times, hindered by God's people. Though there is undeniably always room for maturity and growth, in time, God seeks to bring every person into his/her fullest maturity. As partakers of Christ, we will remain stagnant if we do not learn how to work together in unity among others. When laborers come to stand in the gap where there is a need, we must embrace them and seek ways to preserve our forces. What army refuses help when everyone is fighting for the same cause?

Mark speaks of workers in the vineyard who come in the name of the Lord, but are discarded and awfully mishandled.

> *When the season came, He (God)* **sent a servant** *to the tenants (people of God) to get from them some of the fruit (involvement) of the vineyard (church). And* **they took him** *(the servant) and* **beat him** *and* **sent him away empty-handed**. *Again He (God)* **sent** *to them* **another servant**, *and* **they struck him** *(the servant)* **on the head** *and*

> *treated him shamefully. And He (God)* **sent another,**
> *and* **him they KILLED.** *And so* **with many others: some**
> **they beat,** *and* **some they killed.** (Mark 12:2-5)

Have we ever mistreated or mishandled someone who has genuinely come to help us or others? Perhaps we beat them down with words, slander, gossip, backbiting, or discouragement. Or, maybe we even laughed or scoffed—sending them away shamed, empty-handed, and brokenhearted. The question is, how many have we sent away in this way? How many have we left disoriented or perplexed? Maybe they had something to offer the Body of Christ or something significant to convey as they sincerely sought to contribute to the work of God. How many times have we refused, rebuked, and then rejected a person, accepting only what we want to hear? 2 Timothy 4:3 says, *"For the time will come when people will not put up with sound doctrine. Instead, to suit their own desires, they will gather around them a great number of teachers to say what their itching ears want to hear."*

Do we seek our own way instead of seeking a better way that God is using to challenge and stimulate us for spiritual growth? How many men of God in biblical history have come in the name of the Lord to promote proper worship toward the throne of God—only to be rejected? Before there is true restoration, revival, or maturity, there must be genuine love, holiness, and unity among God's people. Hebrews 12:14 says, *"Work at living in peace with everyone, and work at living a holy life, for those who are not holy will not see the Lord."*

In other words, this means we should seek to be kind to others, even with our words, intentions, and actions. This ensures we do not purposely seek to offend our brothers and sisters—even in secret. We're supposed to be always striving toward the core of God's heart in all things and preserving our purification processes. Have we examined ourselves in self-reflection? A daily walk with God in self-examination is needed. Psalm 51:10 says, *"Create in me a clean heart, O God. Renew a right spirit within me."* No matter what, we all should be bowing our faces and knees down towards God, crying our hearts out for revival.

Our journey with God is not about being popular; it is not about being accepted. It is about loving and encouraging one another, speaking life into one another, speaking the truth concerning what God wants us to deliver, and being sent to help build His temple. Ephesians 4:16 says, *"He makes the whole body fit together perfectly. As each part does its own special work, it helps the other parts grow, so that the whole body is healthy and growing and full of love."* It is imperative for us to follow after God's heart and not our own. Let us not slaughter our servants—preserving each of God's people with encouragement, without malicious intent. Using that approach, we will grow together into full maturity and the work of God will be established (Ephesians 4:13).

Keep the Unity

Unity and courtesy toward others is essential for any group or organization to operate effectively. As long as it does not hinder us from the favor of God or the work of God, let us be sure not to interfere with each other's personal lives and to respect each other's privacy. As we live life, we must also examine our own lives and determine what we can do to improve them. We must avoid unnecessary contentions, gossip, backbiting, slander, and maliciousness.

The apostle Paul spoke openly about the traps and schemes of the enemy—attempting to divide the church in some unseen way. 2 Corinthians 2:11 is where he says, *"Lest Satan should get an advantage of us: for we are not ignorant of his devices."* Likewise, judging others is also an issue we must be watchful of among others. The fact is that we do not know all the details in the lives of others and must consider that we will never fully comprehend what they encounter.

> *Do not judge, or you too will be judged. For in the same way you judge others, you will be judged, and with the measure you use, it will be measured to you. "Why do you look at the speck of sawdust in your brother's eye and pay no attention to the plank in your own eye? How can you say to your brother, 'Let me take the speck out of your eye,' when all the time there is a plank in your own eye?"* (Matthew 7:1-4)

Without a doubt, we are all counseled in some way by our Wonderful Counselor Jesus Christ on a day-to-day basis. Therefore, we must not judge or mistreat one another. We each have our own imperfections and frailties to resolve. Psalm 32:8 says, *"I will instruct you and teach you in the way you should go; I will counsel you with my eye upon you."* Overall, we should know that God will help us all along the way, without allowing our own assumptions or opinions to provoke others. As we pursue the work of God, He will continuously direct us as we go through our individual life experiences.

Chapter 13

PURIFICATION ESSENTIALS

A s we get accustomed to pursuing God's instruction, we are systematically being consecrated and purified. It is a process in which God preserves His people. This is known as a method of purging, sculpting, or shaping through extreme events that God uses to purify us into a holy path of living. Isaiah 64:8 says, *"But now, O LORD, thou art **Our Father**; we are **The Clay,** and thou **Our Potter**; and we **ALL** are **The Work Of Thy Hand**."* At the same time, purification deals with how we value aspects of sanctity and holiness. You, the disciple, must reason with God based on what He desires of you and how it will ultimately benefit your spiritual alignment.

1) Keeping our minds and hearts pure is a vital practice. Valuing our time with God is another dynamic feature of stimulating spiritual growth. Another good quality is lengthening our prayers to yield the best encounter with the Almighty. In this way, we prevent ritualizing prayer by yearning more for a closer experience with God. Seeking His presence and not ending our prayers until His presence is found and felt is important. 1 Chronicles 16:11 says, *"Seek the Lord and His strength, seek His face continually."*

2) Giving God reverence and honor includes bowing down as a sign of respect. We must not lose this tradition in our generation. God responds to humility and reverence. We must be certain that there is no disrespect toward God and that we do not take

Him for granted. According to Christian author Steven Phillips (2018) at Living Word Studies, the word *worship* means *to bow down*.[12] Psalm 95:6 says, *"O come, let us worship and bow down: let us kneel before the LORD our maker."*

Moses experienced the powerful presence of God in Exodus 33:21-22, which says, *"And the LORD said, 'Behold, there is a place by me where you shall stand on the rock, and while **MY GLORY** passes by I will put you in a cleft of the rock, and I will cover you with my hand until I have passed by."*

These are just a few reasons why we should consider bowing before Him not only in our hearts, but also physically bowing down in His presence. As long as we are physically able, bowing is how we should give God the highest honor.

3) We should work cohesively to uplift God's kingdom. As a vessel of God, we should be utilizing various talents, gifts, and skills to form the Body of Christ. In this way, we assist God in developing the fivefold ministry through the Body of Christ within phases of participation and unity. 1 Corinthians 12:20-21 says, *"But now are they many members, yet one body. And the eye cannot say unto the hand, I have no need of thee. The head cannot say unto the feet, I have no need of you."*

Each member is distinct and irreplaceable according to their individuality—fulfilling their God-given tasks and assignments. As leaders, we must permit the flow of God's movement through His people in order to build His church in a healthy and functional manner. This builds a strong core of members and disciples—bringing in newcomers to mentor and releasing them into their ministries.

4) Avoiding what is ungodly is a method of spiritual warfare. It's similar to those who participate in martial arts guarding against or deflecting attacks from an opponent. Whenever the enemy

---

[12] Phillips, S. (2018). *The Mystery Hidden in Shachah: The Hebrew Word for Worship.* Living Word Discovery. Retrieved November 5, 2019 from http://livingwordin3d.com/discovery/2018/02/25/the-mystery-hidden-in-shachah-the-hebrew-word-for-worship/.

attempts to spiritually attack or infiltrate our minds with some sort of negativity, our hearts with impurity, our eyes with lust, our mouths with gossip, or our ears with corruption, we must immediately resist to deflect that attack or influence. We are admonished in 1 Thessalonians 5:22 to, *"Stay away from every kind of evil."*

The more we seek God, the more He reveals the impurities in our lives. It must be our hearts' desire to maintain purity and seek the best interests of our spiritual growth practices. The fact is that we must always be moving toward what is godly. If not, we become stationary targets for the enemy Satan, as he seeks to hinder our purification processes. The way we guard ourselves from evil influence determines how mature we become in the eyes of God. We cannot deliberately sin and please God. Without purification, we will not receive spiritual gifts. We must keep ourselves pure enough to be used.

Spiritual Gifts & Identities

Without question, everyone is meant to live out and accomplish God's divine pleasure. It is a journey that completes who you are and involves a purposeful life that is allocated for each person. Those discoveries are known through spiritual gifts. Spiritual gifts are powers, skills, abilities, or knowledge given by God through the Holy Spirit to Christians (Ephesians 4:11-1, Romans 12:6-8, & 1 Corinthians 12:8-10). Spiritual gifts are identified as the following:

Prophecy – Speaking on behalf of God to the church

Leadership – Leading and governing the church and its functions

Exhortation – Inspiring, encouraging, and counseling the church

Teaching – Training and instructing others with God's Word

Word of Knowledge – Understanding truth and detailed insight related to real-life issues

Word of Wisdom – Discerning biblical truths related to real-life issues

Faith – Absolute confidence in God's power and authority

Healing – Administering divine help and deliverance

Discerning of Spirits – Distinguishing the findings of hidden truths and intentions

Interpretation of Tongues – Understanding divine communication between God's people

Giving – Meeting the needs of the church, its community, and others

Serving – Sacrificing time for the needs of others and the church

However, the enemy is very strategic. He attempts to find ways to throw us off course. The more closely connected we are with the Lord, the more he attacks through people, circumstances, and temptations. But know this...the enemy is trying to prevent us from discovering the true purposes and spiritual identities the Lord has purposed for us. So the questions are these:

1. Which spiritual gifts have been or will be imparted by the hand of God to you?
2. Are you really encountering God the way you should?
3. Have you sought to please God in all you do?
4. Is your lifestyle set apart to serve the Lord at your fullest potential?
5. Have you made an absolute effort to accomplish all God has purposed for you?

In my journey, I have found that if we are willing, God finds a way to raise us up. The Lord does not linger on our mistakes, yet He corrects us. His heart desires us to give Him pleasure from our walk in purity. It is not an overnight process, but a step-by-step journey. Ultimately, God wants spiritual growth in the church. He wants to use those who are willing to be used. Whether you are called to help establish the fivefold ministry, or purposed to be a blessing of support within a church community in any way, just know God is still looking for people to be used. He wants to manifest the gifts of the Spirit. As God is building up His disciples, will you actively seek your true identity? Remember, God wants to birth something through you.

Discover your spiritual identity in the Lord. God wants to bring revival, restoration, and development into the church. God wants to impart spiritual gifts. He wants to raise up mature ministers within the Body of Christ and unveil the working of the Holy Spirit through the fivefold ministry. The fivefold ministry consists of pastors, apostles, prophets, evangelists, and teachers (Ephesians 4:11). We must continue to walk in holiness and earnestly seek after God's counsel and guidance over our lives. As we pursue and make efforts, those of us who do not yet know our calling will suddenly know. Those of us who already know our callings will begin to be encouraged to do more of God's work, if we yield to the power of the Holy Spirit.

Chapter 14

DIVINE VISION FOR
CHURCH STRUCTURE

ow we respond to God's Word and to our callings will yield definitive outcomes: either we will adhere to God's desire for His people or we won't. Nevertheless, a great sense of vision within our church is a great need. In fact, it's vital for the sake of church direction and overall ministry effectiveness. The Body of Christ must remain cohesive when pursuing godly objectives. Each member can take part in unifying the body through utilizing various talents, gifts, or skillsets. As a result of God's leading and our participation, we will be equipped enough to flow within the divine move of God. Let us understand that God is not limited in whatever He plans to do. As the Creator, He purposefully orchestrates experiences and finds methods to equip His people. Suppose you and many others around you made extensive efforts to support your local church enough to make a difference. Imagine the outcome that would stem from those efforts when God is already waiting for your contribution. We, as Christians, would be able to reach communities, cities, regions, or even nations.

However, the pressures and demands of ministry responsibilities can be too much to manage alone. Licensed ministers with Christian International Apostolic Network mention that 1,800 pastors leave the ministry every month due to trying to do too much for their church alone (Starfire Ministries, 2019).[13]

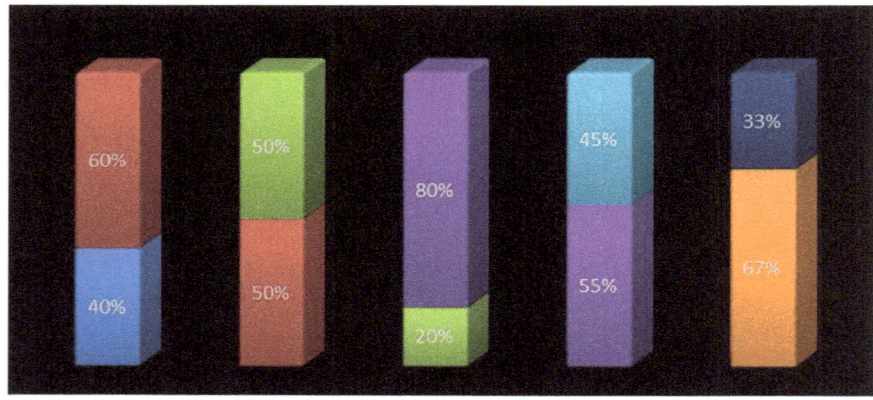

- Forty percent of pastors will not remain in ministry within ten years.
- Fifty percent of pastors felt incapable of meeting the needs of the job.

---

[13] Starfire Ministries (2019). *Do You Know Why Fivefold Ministry is Essential?* Retrieved August 13, 2019 from https://www.starfireministries.org/do-you-know-why-fivefold-ministry-is-essential/.

- Eighty percent believe that pastoral ministry negatively distresses their families.
- Forty-five percent of pastors say they have encountered depression or burnout to the degree they needed a leave of absence from ministry.
- Thirty-three percent felt overwhelmed within their first five years of ministry.

Starfire Ministries further mention that it is impossible to entirely alleviate the pressure that pastors face on a daily basis. To make things worse, the strain is greatly compounded when the fivefold ministry gifts are not fully operating in churches today (Starfire Ministries, 2019). It is not God's intention for pastors to attempt to equip and build up the Body of Christ alone. In fact, the Bible does not even suggest that one person has been given everything necessary to perfect a particular congregation, Starfire Ministries declares. The Bible has made it clear that fivefold ministers are meant to operate within their special giftings and abilities. By doing so, together, they govern, guide, gather, ground, and guard God's people. The Scriptures mention it is a collective effort that not only provides adequate support for pastors, but also stimulates maturity for God's people.

> So **Christ Himself** gave the **Apostles**, the **Prophets**, the **Evangelists**, the **Pastors** and **Teachers**, to **equip** His people for works of service, so that the **Body Of Christ** may be **built up** until we all **reach unity** in the **faith** and in the **knowledge** of **The Son Of God** and **become mature, attaining to the whole measure of the fullness of Christ**. (Ephesians 4:11-13)

Regardless of the many pressures of ministry, there is a spiritual unfolding of possibilities. As we have seen from the Scriptures, God Himself has given us a layout of how pulpit ministry should be orchestrated. Below are a few specifics related to church structure that we, as a church, could perhaps consider when building God's kingdom. Those details are as follows:

1) **Vision** – The enemy Satan is very strategic in the way he attempts to find ways to throw God's people off course. The more closely we find connection with the Lord, the more he attacks through people, circumstances, and divisions. For that reason, it is imperative that we as the Body of Christ are not deterred from discovering the true purposes and spiritual identities the Lord has purposed for us. As one in Christ, God's people ought to sincerely encourage those efforts.

2) **Fivefold Ministry** – A healthy church consists of these essential ministerial gifts operating in the church. According to Christian Truth Center (2016), "A congregation without an apostle is self-willed, blind without a prophet, ingrown without an evangelist, numb without a teacher, and spoiled with only the pastor." God can still move even if the church is not governed by the fivefold ministry, but the church will not be as effective and progressive as it was meant to be.

Apostle – Administration that governs by laying a foundation with proper doctrinal and spiritual structure

Prophet – Exhorts, leads, warns, and identifies with the purposes of God

Pastor – Guides, protects, cares for, and commits to the church

Teacher – Grounds, instructs, and directs the church in biblical truth

Evangelist – Participates in outreach, witnesses, and wins souls for Christ and the church

3) **Role Fulfillment** – Through one's pursuit of divine purpose, God can place His people systematically within the Body of Christ to carry out His own measure of glory. As a result of this fulfillment, men and women alike are empowered by God for service to do His work within the church.

4) **Organization** – Establishing roles and functions within the Body of Christ is highly useful in efforts to spread God's glory upon the earth through His people. Discipleship programs, workshops, or fellowship e-groups should perhaps be available— designed to assist members through their learning processes, through both Scripture and holy lifestyle practices. Once this development is functional, the delegation of responsibilities can also be applied.

5) **Involvement** – God desires participation in building His church. He wants to manifest the gifts of the Spirit within His people. He yearns to make a person that was once uncertain certain that he/she has significance. And the only way to find out where we belong is to search for what God has for us. In

that, God methodically raises us up, as we avoid complacency and make ourselves available.

6) **Support** – Leaders and members should be encouraging one another and lifting up the next person. It's not about you or me, but it's about us. Together we can move many obstacles and manage various issues as they arise. No army should desire to live in isolation or somehow remain divided from their own troops. In the same way, we must welcome those who come to help as well as those who are in need.

7) **Relationship** – This means meeting the needs of people, being of service to one another, sharing hurts, and preserving peace between others. It is allowing our hearts to forgive during potential moments of misunderstanding or wrongdoing. Not being selfish or self-centered as we help others before we help ourselves which is a sign of mature and upright behavior. In essence, it's about connection.

8) **Unity** – Life is not all about us, but it is about those around us and God's purpose for all. Without unity, a team cannot accomplish their goals. A strong army always moves in the same direction. A unified people can accomplish huge objectives. Without it, we are depleted.

9) **Revival** – We should be pursuing an outpouring of the Holy Spirit during the overflow of God's presence. That is precisely what we will discover when we come to unity of the faith. It is a place in the Spirit where God's people are aligned with Him in a special way. If you want to truly see God move, establish harmony in the church and allow God's people to operate as they were meant to function.

God absolutely desires this accomplishment within the church. Jesus said He will build a church and the gates of hell would not prevail against it (Matthew 16:18, KJV). However, this has a lot to do with leaders thoroughly delegating and releasing workers into some sort of ministry for the church, not doing it all by themselves—allowing God to establish various callings within the churches. 2 Peter 1:10 says, *"Therefore, brothers, be all the more diligent to confirm your calling and election, for if you practice these qualities you will never fall."*

God is raising up men and women, releasing them, and using them to reach out to others. The primary reason for the Gospel of Jesus Christ is to save souls and stimulate spiritual development (1 Peter 4:6). Let us continue to press toward the movement of God by submitting our determinations entirely. Being made in God's image, He made each individual for a specific purpose to live out that spiritual pursuit. Identifying with our sense of vision is essential when dealing with church infrastructure.[14] Irrefutably, God has good things in store for us if we remain faithful and diligent to service. Philippians 1:6 says, *"For I am confident of this very thing, that He who began a good work in you will perfect it until the day of Christ Jesus."*

---

[14]   Walker, P.L. (2000*). Learning the Practices of Ministry.* Church of God School of Ministry. Cleveland, Tennessee.

CONCLUDING WORDS OF WISDOM

E veryone can live a meaningful life, and I would like to leave you with these words. As humans, we live, we learn, and we assimilate into our environment according to our experiences. But one thing for certain is that God made us to do something great within those phases of life. Within that arrangement, He has orchestrated strategies for us to succeed. Not long ago, I was going through a few things at work and in ministry. I was offended, frustrated, and looking to God for answers. God revealed to me we should follow three fundamental principles daily.

1) Love those that do not deserve it.
2) Be thankful for what you have.
3) Do what you are supposed to do.

First, love those that do not deserve it. Many times when people offend us, it is not so easy to forgive. However, we are commanded to do so. Jesus said in John 15:10, *"If ye keep my commandments, ye shall abide in my love; even as I have kept my Father's commandments, and abide in his love."* Jesus also said in Matthew 5:44, *"But I say to you, Love your enemies and pray for those who persecute you, Love those that do not deserve it."*

Next, we should always be thankful for what we have in life. Oftentimes, we think our situation is worse than the next person's, or that we are the only ones going through certain problems or extreme circumstances. But later, we find out that others are going through the same adversities or may, in some cases, be less privileged than we are. We must realize that no one has a perfect life; we all have to deal with some difficulties. 1 Thessalonians 5:18 says, *"Give thanks in all circumstances; for this is the will of God in Christ Jesus for you."* Colossians 4:2 says, *"Devote yourselves to prayer, being watchful and thankful."*

Third, we should do what we are supposed to do. If we are not careful, we can easily miss an opportunity to grow spiritually. Doing what is right is ideal, as God acknowledges when we make that extra effort to do what we are supposed to do. Titus 2:12 says, *"We are to renounce ungodliness and worldly passions, and to live self-controlled, upright, and godly lives in this present time."* Hebrews 13:16 says, *"But to do good (which is to do what is right) and to communicate forget not: for with such sacrifices God is well pleased."*

I encourage us all to love those that do not deserve it, be thankful for what we have, and do what we are supposed to do—seeking God fervently with a sincere heart of submission. We can always point fingers at the next person, but we must first do what is required of us. Do what is honorable in the sight of God. The Bible says, *"He who overcomes shall inherit all things and I will be their God and they will be my people"* (Revelation 21:7, CEV).

BIOGRAPHY

Prophet Floyd Brown II is a Christian encouragement writer and the founder of Holy Manifestation Ministries, which began in Baltimore, Maryland. Brown is married with five children. He was first called by God into ministry in the year 2000 and has been a spiritual developer for various churches over the years. Brown earned a master's degree in psychology from the University of the Rockies, accomplished study in ministry at Calling & Ministries Studies (CAMS) in Roanoke, Virginia, and acquired training from Apostolic Movement International (AMI), established in San Diego, California. With a heart for discipleship, Brown assists members with discovering their purposes within the Body of Christ. He has served on the church board as council member and spiritual leader with the Christian foundational organization Church of God Ministries in Northern Virginia.

As an elder, Brown provides essential functions such as facilitating intercessory prayer and providing supportive pulpit ministry for the congregation. In efforts to enhance church functions, Brown now assists elders in various church organizations with the fundamentals of spiritual development and prayer, while administering exhortation, teaching, and preaching. Brown has a deep burden within to help God's people. With a call from God as the driving force, he has applied that vision not only into public exhortation, but also into literature in a divine mission to build up those who need encouragement and to reinforce those who desire the deeper things of God.

Growing Up

In his early years as a child, Brown was born and raised in a Holy Ghost-filled Pentecostal church (Faith Tabernacle) in Baltimore, Maryland. At age thirteen, he began to fall away from the Lord. He then began hanging out with the unsaved as he tried to fit in with longtime neighborhood friends. To make the situation even worse, he stopped attending church and eventually lost his connection with God. Becoming somewhat of a troubled teen, misguided and uncertain about life, he often sought direction.

When he was eighteen, he was asked by a close friend, Darick Harris, to meet him at a local house party in Baltimore, Maryland. Within a few minutes of arriving, a fight broke out in front of the house in the street. His close friend Darick was shot—along with two other longtime friends (Charles Jones and Anthony Holman). Simultaneously, he and several others were also fired upon and forced to duck between cars and trees to prevent being shot. Floyd went home that night with Darick's blood on his face.

The next day, a Sunday morning, Brown's close friend Darick passed away. It was a life-changing moment for Floyd. Saddened, he did a lot of soul-searching, and his hanging out days ended. He began to focus on a career and decided to join the United States Marines. Finally, at age twenty-four, he enlisted and found himself in a world of adversity through the United States Marine boot camp training. Being punched and spit on by drill instructors, recruits experienced a hard life. In these moments during training, Floyd once again recognized the significance of needing God in his life. At times, he held a cross in his hands before going to sleep.

Shortly after Marine Corps boot camp ended, Brown found out that one of his drill instructors that graduated his platoon shot himself in front of fifty-nine recruits on their sixth day of training at the swim qualification (Paris Island, South Carolina, 1994). At this time, Brown did some self-reflection in relation to his true purpose. He realized his drill instructor, in some way, was supposed to be a mentor—yet he had neither real peace nor true direction. Still, Brown continued to live his life without seeking God—just living daily life without further considering his past experiences, church roots, or Christian beliefs.

The Call into Ministry

When he was thirty, Brown was watching the (1999) movie, "The Ten Commandments." After the movie ended, all of a sudden, he felt the presence of God very intensely. Being raised up in church, he knew what that presence felt like. Even though he was a hard-faced Marine at that time, tears rolled uncontrollably down his face. Then, for the first time ever, he heard God's voice. God said, "I want to use you to help and strengthen my people, like Moses." Brown then internally replied to God that he was not capable of being used in that way. God's presence just lingered.

God said, "Enough is enough…it's time for you to know who you really are." He told Brown, "You had enough wallowing in your mistakes. You got all of that play out of you…now I'm calling you out of this world. I am calling you into ministry. Your true purpose is not a United States Marine…your true purpose is not a law-enforcement officer. You are a man of God. I am not calling you into the warfare of the land. I am calling you into the warfare of the air."

It was then, in 1999, when Brown first understood what his true purpose in life was and what he was supposed to pursue. Days later, Elder Andrew Henry (now his mentor) of Emmanuel Apostolic Tabernacle, invited him to church where, four months later, Brown was baptized by the Holy Ghost at a local church revival in Baltimore. Brown began ministering under this apostolic movement, as God prepared him for further ministry.

The Vision and the Dream

The vision for this book began early in his call into ministry around 2001. God gave him this biblical message to preserve in a safe place, as if it had some great significance. It was derived from Habakkuk 2:1: *"I will take my stand at my watchpost and station myself on the tower, and look out to see what he will say to me, and what I will answer concerning my complaint. And the LORD answered me, and said, Write the vision, and make it plain upon tables, that he may run that readeth it."*

In addition, by 2002, Brown had a dream of a marvelous cross. After awakening, he realized what he saw in his dream could be something created. In fact, he knew it would be a way to glorify God and to create a business. From time to time, he thought about it but at that stage in life took no further action.

Preparation for Ministry

However, preparation for ministry intensified. God began to tell Floyd about his calling in ministry and that He would soon suffer like the man named Job in the Bible (Job 2-36). Brown even told his mentor, Elder Andrew Henry, that God was constantly directing him to the book of Job. His mentor responded by confirming that Brown would most likely face extreme suffering. Then, all of a sudden, Brown encountered various, unfortunate events:

1) He suffered instant financial turmoil and isolation.
2) He could not see his children as he desired due to spousal contentions.
3) His character was slandered with false accusations.
4) He could no longer afford his car, and it was repossessed in front of his coworkers.
5) He lost his friends.
6) He was laughed at and mocked.

7) He was rejected by people, as if he had leprosy.

8) He was shunned and mistreated.

9) He was ignored by people he loved.

10) He was the object of backbiting and gossip.

11) His new apartment had a flea infestation.

12) He often didn't have a dime in his pocket.

13) He was hungry.

14) He was viciously hated by people for little or no reason.

Through many tribulations, various trials, and numerous adversities, Floyd developed a deep relationship with God...it was during this time when Brown ultimately learned how to rely on and trust in God, no matter what happens. Under these circumstances and conditions, Brown encountered a very close connection with God and was able to feel a portion of the sufferings of Jesus. Since then, God has restored him. So over the years, whenever he experiences suffering, he certainly remembers the source of his help. Without a doubt, Brown has also recognized that man can neither help nor save himself—ONLY the sovereign and merciful God can preserve mankind.

The Holy Wooden Cross

By 2006, God spoke to Brown, urging him to find the materials to make the cross he had seen in his dream. He wrestled with God about the idea of crafting such an item, because he had never been a craftsman. Nevertheless, God told him to go and the work would be anointed. As he entered the store, attempting to find the materials necessary for this project, he was amazed when he began to find each piece needed from various departments of the store. Returning home with his tools and material, he proceeded to construct this cross. Three hours later, the divinely inspired hand-made cross was finished. However, a few items were missing that had been seen in his dream, so the project was once again put on hold.

In 2014, after Prophet Brown assisted with ministering practices at a local church function in Lorton, Virginia, a stranger (Ron Bauzon) walked up to him. He confirmed with Brown in the spirit what his calling in ministry was and how he was to operate for the churches. Then the stranger also said, "You have a business." Brown replied that, at one time, he had been working on something in the past. Bauzon replied, "No...you have a business."

So Brown began to pray concerning this business, and God directed him to further pursue the wooden cross project revealed years earlier. He began searching for the missing items he had seen in his dream, and after about a week, he had what he needed to complete the product. Since then, Brown has been constructing these crosses to give Jesus glory and to share with those who will also honor what God has done.

Holy Manifestation Ministries

Brown was aware of the prophetic call on his life from the epiphany he experienced with the Lord and through the discernment of various ministers. But he had no inkling that God would later send him to college for six years to earn a master's degree in psychology to enhance his writing abilities. As a result, Prophet Brown has combined his vision to write Christian encouragement books and handcraft these wooden crosses to glorify God and to exhibit the wonders of God. He inspires others to give pleasure to God through a keen sense of obedience and perseverance. Brown also invites others to enjoy with him these marvelous God-given products made through the hand of God and His leading. May the Lord be with you and may the Lord be glorified! The Holy Handmade Cross can be viewed online:

Facebook at Leah Plus Floyd
More details on Prophet Floyd Brown's ministry visit floydjbrown.com
Twitter: Holy Manifestation Ministries (@HolyManifest1) and
Email Address: holy.manifestation.ministries@gmail.com

Prophet Brown's focus is to pursue the heart of God and to ensure that God's people are seeking their God-given purposes to establish a greater sense of fulfillment in their lives. Assisting churches with discipleship, organizational structure platforms, and intercessory prayer, as well as winning souls for Christ are at the core of Brown's assignment for the Lord to help God's people reach a deeper place, a higher place, in Him.

MORE TESTIMONIALS

"Your ministry has blessed me tremendously because of your words of encouragement influenced by the Holy Spirit. Although I'm by myself pastoring a church, watching your videos and reading your sermons has inspired me to continue to preach, teach, sing, and play music for the Lord. God bless you, Brother Prophet."

Pastor Dwayne Williams

"This is awesome. I've been touched deeply by your teaching. So much of what you have said has been confirmation for me. Thank you for all your prayers and revelations. God bless you, my brother."

Arnetha Rambus

"Often when I'm thinking God is not seeing what I'm going through, I open Facebook and see your posts. They let me know God knows exactly what is happening...it encourages me and gives me the strength to endure it. It hasn't ceased, but through God's Word and people, I have peace knowing He'll fight the battle. I have to learn to trust, be still, and keep my mouth shut! The last being my biggest struggle! Thankful for you being obedient! Amen!"

Tavara Kountz

"Shalom, you have been an inspiration in my life while I have been on a journey where man had no hope for my life. You have come alongside me spiritually, a distance away, and sharpened iron with me, and by doing that, it helped me to be more determined with my faith in a way that is persistent in never giving up."

Sylvia Dawn

First of all, I want to thank our Lord for the life of Brother Floyd. We attended the same church back 2015. He is appreciated for being a good encourager and great leader as our Intercessory Prayer facilitator. I really felt the moving of the mighty power of God from his life. So blessed also for all the inspiring email messages he would send our church members. I pray that God will continue to work in his life. May God continue to bless him and his family.

Cristina Trinidad

"Thank you, Floyd Brown, for all your encouraging Facebook posts and prophetic videos. Thank you for taking the time to post messages that help me grow. You have been an inspiration to me. I greatly appreciate your cooperation with the Holy Spirit. You once gave me a prophetic word that changed me and gave me reassurance that Jesus was calling me into the ministry. I appreciate you and all you do to help us mature."

Jessie Drake

"Your words really do inspire me. I truly feel that they are coming from the Lord."

LaKeitha Denese Culpepper

"As we commit to pursuing His presence, He will
commit His presence upon us."